PLAYING THE GAME

PLAYING THE GAME
Christine Poulter

MACMILLAN

First published 1987

Published by
Higher and Further Education Division
MACMILLAN PUBLISHERS LTD
Houndmills, Basingstoke, Hampshire RG21 2XS
and London
Companies and representatives
throughout the world

Typeset by Wessex Typesetters
(Division of The Eastern Press Ltd)
Frome, Somerset

British Library Cataloguing in Publication Data
Poulter, Christine
Playing the game.
1. Acting
I. Title
792′.028   PN2061
ISBN 0–333–40384–3
ISBN 0–333–40385–1 Pbk

CONTENTS

LIST OF ILLUSTRATIONS   vi

PREFACE   vii

ACKNOWLEDGEMENTS   viii

HOW TO USE THIS BOOK   1

INTRODUCTION   3

NOTES FOR STUDENTS   4

1 WARM-UP GAMES   24

2 OBSERVATION GAMES   51

3 ENCOUNTER GAMES   80

4 IMPROVISATION GAMES   101

5 WORD AND STORY GAMES   130

INDEX OF GAMES   151

LIST OF ILLUSTRATIONS

High Focus – an unwilling victim 5
Low Focus 6
Shared High Focus 7
Passing High Focus 8
Volunteer High Focus 8
High Focus 9
Granny's Footsteps 12
Pirate's Gold 12
Guard and Thief 13
Organizing 16
Applause 28
Distractions 35
Granny's Footsteps 37
Quick Feelings 48
Strings 49
Mirrors 69
Pirate's Gold 72
Spot the Difference 75
Blind Trust 86
Guard and Thief 89
Trust Circle 99
Cliffhanger 107
Grand Opera 111
Hot Seat 114
Thinks and Says 124
Touching Scene 125
Triangles 127
Final Frame 138
Photo News 148
Picture Book 149

PREFACE

Actors preparing a role need to use their powers of observation and creativity. When performing the role on stage in front of an audience they need a whole range of presentational skills and plenty of self-confidence.

Directors and drama teachers often use games and exercises in the rehearsal/workshop situation to develop such skills, which are not only relevant to the drama and theatre world. If 'All the world's a stage' and everyone, at some time, is faced with situations which call for self-confidence and effective presentation (e.g. a job interview or committee meeting) then they too could benefit from preparation through the use of similar games and exercises.

Although written primarily for directors, drama teachers and drama students, this book will also be of use to anyone working with a group of people on the development of skills such as observation, imagination, presentation and self-confidence.

C.P.

Christine Poulter was Lecturer in Drama and Theatre Arts at the University of Birmingham and is now Drama Officer for Yorkshire Arts.

ACKNOWLEDGEMENTS

The author would like to acknowledge the following for their help: Carry Goorney and Interplay, Steve Trow and Jubilee Theatre, Imelda Foley and Northern Ireland Arts Council, Bernard and Mary Laughlin and the Tyrone Guthrie Centre, Annaghmakerrig, David Hirst, Sarah Mahaffy and, most of all, Tom Magill. In addition, I thank Tom Scott for his illustrations for the book.

Acknowledgement is also due to Jocelyn Powell, adviser, teacher and friend, who died in September 1986 and to whom this book is dedicated.

HOW TO USE THIS BOOK

Directors and teachers

Experienced directors or teachers are likely to be searching for new material, not seeking advice on how to run a session. Such readers should feel free to proceed to the main body of the book, the games themselves. Terms used throughout the book are explained below.

Students and those new to drama games

Although the purpose of this book is to provide step-by-step instructions for the playing of 100 games, there are some skills needed by a director which are acquired through practice rather than instruction. I have included a short section of advice for students – lessons which I have learned over the years as I have evolved my own method of working. I have included the section as a reference only – directors and teachers develop their own ways of dealing with problems and structuring activities. The best teacher is experience.

Terms used in the instructions for playing the games:

NUMBERS. The games are numerically coded. The first digit refers to the section of the book in which the game can be found. The second and third digits refer to its number within that section.

> *Prefix*: 1XX = Warm-up games
> 2XX = Observation games
> 3XX = Encounter games
> 4XX = Improvisation games
> 5XX = Word and story games

At the beginning of each game is a diagram of the game plus a summary of facts about the game under the following headings:

FOCUS. Throughout the book I have included the term FOCUS as an indication of the confidence needed by the player(s). The use of Focus as a means of building self-confidence is dealt with under Notes for Students. FOCUS in this context refers to the attention being paid to the player. Is s/he the focus of

1

attention? Is everyone else watching? If a game is LOW FOCUS the answer is no – probably only a partner is focusing on any one player as all the others are playing the game at the same time. If a game is HIGH FOCUS the answer is yes, everyone else is audience watching the solitary player.

Volunteer high focus indicates high focus games involving an audience/performer relationship within which the player has chosen to take the focus by volunteering to be the solitary player.

Shared high focus indicates that although the player is being watched, s/he is not alone as there are two or more players at any time.

Passing high focus games actively involve everyone but at any one time the group is focusing on only one person. As indicated by the word PASSING, this focus moves quickly onto another member of the group, for example by the throwing of a ball, so that no-one has to endure the focus for too long.

SHAPE. The SHAPE of each game is described to help the session leader who wishes to avoid the organizational problems involved in rearranging a group from a circle into teams, into partners and so on. A quick glance at the SHAPE description enables the leader to choose appropriate games for the space, number in the group and so on.

INTRODUCTION

TIME. I have included a guide to the time needed to play each game as a help to session leaders trying to plan a session to fit a specific time allocation.

The first figure represents the minimum time needed to play the game. The second figure represents the time that could be allowed if the game is to be played to the full.

I have not allowed time for setting-up or practising the game within this allocation. As you become familiar with the games you will adapt these times to suit your version of the game.

ENERGY. Some games need a large empty space, others need tolerant neighbours if players are running around at speed or shouting very loudly. I have tried to indicate the level of physical or vocal energy required for each game; mental and creative energy are not implied in the level indicated.

SHOW. This refers to the performance potential of the game. Some games already include a performance element but others can be used as performance exercises – the performance occurring before, after or instead of the whole-group version of the game. Some games are unsuitable for performance and are noted as such.

EXTRAS. Most of the games require only a working space and a group of players. Some require a few props/materials such as blindfolds or footballs. Even these games, with the exception of two, can be played without the specified materials. Players can close their eyes if they have no blindfolds and throw a soft object if there is no football.

NOTES FOR STUDENTS

The following section comprises thoughts and advice that I
have compiled over the years in response to questions about
the skills required of the session leader. I am still learning all
the time and would expect any student to add to this summary
from their own experience.

BUILDING THE GROUP

Confidence

Confidence is always a difficult issue to tackle in a group
situation. Directors and drama teachers often assume that their
actors/students have plenty of confidence but this is not always
true. Most people only have confidence when doing something
they can manage quite easily and often lose it when faced with
a new task or experience. The task of the session leader is to
work in a way which develops the self-confidence of everyone
in the group.

Many games assist group development by helping players to
get to know each other and to feel relaxed in each other's
company. All games played in pairs give people the chance to
talk on a one-to-one basis. A session of these, in which the
leader ensures that no-one goes to the same partner twice, can
be an excellent ice-breaker.

With adult groups, games that remind them of their own
childhood play, for example WHAT'S THE TIME MR WOLF?, or
those which are very physical and seem silly such as KNEE
FIGHTS, are marvellous for awakening an instant sense of
energy and fun – essential ingredients for successful play.

The games in the Encounter section of this book are
specifically concerned with developing trust and support within
the group.

Careful planning can ensure that a player's self-confidence is
not shattered at an early stage. This can happen if a player is
placed in a HIGH FOCUS situation before s/he is ready for it.

Focus

In the same way that an audience focuses its attention on the players, so the players should focus their attention on the task in hand – namely their performance. Players' awareness of the audience can be counter productive if it is so great that it distracts them from their performance. Little will be learned except about the power of stage fright.

There is safety in numbers and an individual performer can feel more secure when performing as part of a group. The solitary player is in what I term a HIGH FOCUS situation, that is s/he is the focus of everybody's attention. If s/he did not volunteer for this position s/he will most probably be terrified, which in turn can lead to underachievement. This fear will only serve to reinforce a reluctant approach to the situation in the future.

HIGH FOCUS – an unwilling victim.

The session leader can and often does rely on the willing volunteer or the confident player, a strategy which should be used sparingly if other members of the group are ever to attempt the solo spot.

It is possible to build a player's confidence through the use of LOW FOCUS games, for example those played in pairs.

LOW FOCUS

Here there can be many solitary players playing to an audience of one, their partner. This is such a low focus situation that players tend to forget the performer/audience relationship and concentrate on the task in hand.

Having tried a low focus game, the same game can be used as a demonstration to the rest of the group. Alternatively an improvisation exercise can be performed by three or four players rather than one or two. The focus on each player will be higher than in the partner exercise but at least it is shared.

SHARED HIGH FOCUS

As a player's confidence and experience of taking the focus
develops s/he may be encouraged to be a solitary player. One
way of giving players a taste of high focus without the problem
of having to sustain it is to use games in which the focus
passes quickly around the group as it would in a ball game.

PASSING HIGH FOCUS

The focus is on one player at a time but is passing from player to player. Given time and practice most players will have the self-confidence to volunteer for a high focus situation which has to be sustained for longer than a few seconds.

VOLUNTEER HIGH FOCUS

This should save the session leader from always having to choose the player for high focus work from within an unwilling group. The aim should be that all players attain the self-confidence needed to sustain a high focus performance whether as a volunteer or as a selected performer.

HIGH FOCUS

PLANNING THE SESSION

It is worth spending some time in advance planning a possible programme for a session. This allows you to consider how best to achieve the aims of the session and how best to ensure that each game or exercise used constitutes a step towards your attempted goal.

Warm-up

When you walk into a room to take a session you are faced with a group of people who are all thinking about or doing different things. The energy level varies from person to person

– some are running wild, others look as if they would rather be asleep. You must work for concentration right from the start of the session, helping the group to forget what is happening outside the room.

Not only do you want them to concentrate, you also want them to put energy and interest into their time with you. Unfortunately, if you were to say 'Stop playing – it's time for work' those who had been running wild would think that they must stop being energetic and having fun and should adopt a more serious working attitude. If you can utilize that energy they will get a lot more out of the session.

In the same way, if you launch straight into the main part of your work, those who are half-asleep at the outset will miss the point of the first five minutes and be left behind. If you spend five minutes waking them up they too will get a lot more from the session.

A warm-up is one answer to these problems and is worth planning for the beginning of any session. The purpose is to use up some of the energy in those who are running wild while waking up those who are half-asleep. At the end of a warm-up everybody should be saying 'What's next?' and be ready to tackle it.

A warm-up is any game or exercise which prepares the group for work. It should require some physical energy and be exciting or interesting so that the group starts to have fun. The aim is that the group should want to pause for breath at the end of the warm-up – the perfect state in which to listen to you.

The choice of exercise depends on the number of people and the size of your working space. For drama work it is usual for players to wear loose, comfortable clothes and I would advise non-drama groups to wear the same.

Practice: Any game can be spoilt for the players if they are not clear about the rules. Whenever you are planning to use a complicated game or one which requires a particular skill it is worth allowing time for practice before starting the game.

Blindfolds: Allow time for the group to explore the space while wearing blindfolds. They will soon realize that all low, hard or sharp surfaces must be approached with care. Even after a practice it is advisable to keep a vigilant eye as a game proceeds in order to protect those who may, because of the dynamics of the game, move at speed towards dangerous areas of the room.

With a large group it is advisable to plan for three or four players to be free throughout the game to join you as guardians. This duty can be rotated with players removing their blindfolds while assisting you and replacing them to rejoin the game. A lot can be learned by watching how people move without the aid of sight.

Throwing: Some people lack confidence in their ability to throw and catch a ball. Others are so nervous or enthusiastic about the game that they become careless with this simple action. Once again it is worth allowing time for a practice in your plans. You will probably find that players are more worried about catching than they are about throwing – yet a careless throw is often the cause of a bad catch. Place the emphasis on the throwing and you should notice an improvement.

Sequence: In the same way that you allow time for the practice of particular skills before a game, you can plan a sequence of games in which each game acts as the preparation for the next. In the following sequence the games have been planned in this way.

The final game is to be GUARD AND THIEF, an encounter game requiring both blindfolds and stealth. It will be a high focus situation for both the players, with the rest of the group watching their encounter. It can be ruined by shuffling, whispering or giggling from around the room. The two players must believe that the group's interest is engaged in their struggle; absolute silent concentration is required.

In order to practise the listening and blindfold skills, the observation game PIRATE'S GOLD is to be played before GUARD AND THIEF. Even this requires its own preparation as the players have to move silently whilst the Pirate listens for their every movement.

The session actually starts with the warm-up game of GRANNY'S FOOTSTEPS.

GRANNY'S FOOTSTEPS

This game, which many players remember from their
childhood, prepares the group for careful, quiet, controlled
movements. It also prepares them for the next game, PIRATE'S
GOLD.

PIRATE'S GOLD

This game still requires that one player stands at a distance
from the group. It still requires the group, three at a time, to
creep up on the solitary player. That much they are used to,
having practised in the previous game. The difference here is

in the way they are caught. The Pirate is blindfolded and must rely on hearing and not on sight to detect the thieves. The Pirate points towards a sound as opposed to calling a name.

The fact that the whole group was involved in GRANNY'S FOOTSTEPS means that those waiting their turn are not shuffling about or making noises, having become used to moving quietly. They are part of the team that tries to defeat the Pirate and defeat requires silence.

This is followed by GUARD AND THIEF.

GUARD AND THIEF

By now the group can sustain the silence needed to be the 'wall' around the two players. The two players should not feel isolated before an audience as they are continuing a process that has involved the whole group from the start.

The session could then end with the acting exercise in which two players, without blindfolds, re-enact the situation, imagining themselves to be in a completely unlit space. With open eyes they should try to recapture and present the same sense of sightlessness.

RUNNING THE SESSION

Shape

With some groups the business of finding a partner, forming a team, standing in a line or sitting in a circle seems to take an eternity and can be the bane of a session leader's life. Best friends can also be a hindrance in that they tend to stick together and gain more interest from each other than from the work in hand.

When asking people to find a partner add the instruction 'and sit down with your partner'. The stragglers can then be sorted out as they are literally left standing. If you wish to prevent permanent partnerships add the instruction 'and make sure that your partner is someone you haven't worked with before/today/this week'.

Teams tend to have uneven numbers if the group is asked simply to form teams. Ask for small groups, the number in each group being equal to the number of teams you require. Each group must assign letters to its members – A, B, C and so on. Then all the A's go to one end of the room and become team A, all B's become team B, and so on. This system has the added benefit of splitting up friends who were inevitably the components of each small group.

If you want a circle of players facing outwards, ask the group to form a circle facing inwards. They can then turn to face outwards; for some reason players find it difficult to form a circle with their backs to each other.

If you wish to move to small group work after a partner game ask each pair to join up with another. If this results in one spare pair split them up, placing one each amongst the others so there are two groups of five, the rest being of four.

Presentation

All session leaders have their own presentational styles but usually cover a number of points in the setting up of each game:

Aim. Why are we playing this game? However simplistic this question may seem, players like to know why they are playing any game, especially when it constitutes part of their work in perhaps a rehearsal. There is no need to explain every aspect of your reasons for choosing the game; GRANNY'S

14

FOOTSTEPS need not be introduced as an exercise in controlled movement, the players will be satisfied that it is an initial warm-up.

Shape. It is easier to explain the mechanics of a game if the visual aid provided by the shape has already been set up. In GRANNY'S FOOTSTEPS, I tell all the group to stand at one end of the room, then find a volunteer to leave the group and stand at the opposite end. I then explain the game.

Checking the preparation. The physical organization of the group often needs reviewing. Someone is without a partner, the circle looks like a square, and so on. A quick check should be made that everyone is ready to proceed with the game.

Setting up the game/rules of the game. Explain how the game is played. Sometimes setting-up is required before the rules are explained. For example in FRUIT BOWL every player is first given the name of a fruit.

Improving the game. Improvements can be made either before or after playing the game. If a game becomes boring, dangerous or chaotic the session leader should not feel afraid to announce measures which will refine and improve the game. With experience these notes can be made in advance and may be included in the rules next time around.

The following example describes the way in which I might set up the first three games with a new group. It is intended as an illustration of the points made above, not as a script to be learned verbatim.

For two of the games, the first and third, I have indicated the points being made throughout the game. In the second game you can try to identify these for yourself. The games are KNEE FIGHTS (113), GUESS THE LEADER (209), CATCH THE NAME (304).

Aim	*Right, let's get started. Before we do anything too complicated we'll loosen up a bit and get our*
Shape	*bodies working. So . . . find a partner and a space in the room then I'll show you what to do.*

There will be a general hubbub as players find partners and spaces and automatically start chatting. If you stand on a chair or a table you can see over their heads and they can see and hear you more easily.

ORGANIZING

If this is the first time you have asked the players to find a
partner they may just stand and look around. Hurry them along
and perhaps comment *'Come on . . . it's not that difficult to find
a partner but you do have to move. Every time I say find a
partner at least start moving or we'll never get around to playing
the game.'* When everybody has found a partner you can issue
instructions from your perch. First check that everyone has a
partner and has found a space.

Checking	Who hasn't got a partner? There's someone else over here (or . . . join on with one of the pairs and play as a threesome). Move out and make sure that you've got enough space.
Setting up the game	Right! There are only two things you need to know for this game so watch me carefully. First of all put your hands on your knees like this. (You demonstrate). *Those are guarded knees.* Everyone got that? Good. Now take your hands off your knees. (You demonstrate.) *And those are unguarded knees.*
Rules	The aim of the game is to score five points on your partner's unguarded knees. Try and touch their

*knees with your hands but remember that leaves
your knees unguarded so be very careful.*

Before you let them try with each other may I give a word of
warning. Some players are so defensive that they just stand
opposite each other with their hands on their knees, refusing to
move until their partner does so. Although this may be good
tactics it means that they do not loosen up at all, so it is best to
say something about it in advance.

Improving *By the way, there's one special rule. I know and you
the game know that if you stand with guarded knees for the
whole game you can't lose. This is true but it is also
very boring, so I have invented an anti-boredom
rule which is – if you don't move your hands in the
first thirty seconds you're out. It's an attacking
game so, get ready and off you go.*

It does not really matter whether anyone scores five or not as
long as they have run around and had a laugh. I usually let
them play for half a minute or so and then move on to a
variation of the game which I call SWORD FIGHTS.

Develop *Alright! Alright! Stop! Did anyone get to five? four?
three? two? one? Let's try a different one then. Put
one hand behind your back and make sure that the
hand of that arm is in the small of your back. That's
your target. (You demonstrate). Now point one
finger of your other hand. (You demonstrate).
That's your sword. The idea is to try to hit your
partner's target with your sword. First one to five
wins. You mustn't change swords – that's
confusing the enemy and not allowed. If your
partner moves the target hand then that is cheating
so you still aim for the small of the back, O.K.?
Right – get ready and go!*

When they've played for a minute or so ask again who has
scored five, four, three, two and one. The group should now be
warmed up and ready to get on with the main part of the
session.

*Is everyone warmed up now? You'd better sit down and
have a rest. Let's sit in a circle. Move round and make sure
there are no gaps or lumps.
To give us a breather let's play a game which needs lots of
concentration but not too much energy!*

First of all, I'm going to start an action and you are all to copy it so if I beat on the floor you all beat on the floor. If I clap my hands you all clap your hands. Let's try it.

Have a short practice before you continue with the game.

That's fine. Now this time I'm going to keep changing the action and you must copy as soon as you notice the new action. At the moment anyone who walked in would know that I'm the leader because you're all staring at me so when we try it this time don't look at me so obviously. (Practice). Right. Let's try it for real. We need one person to go and stand outside the door. They mustn't peep or listen while we choose a leader. As soon as we're copying the leader the person waiting outside comes back and stands in the middle of the circle. They have to try and guess who the leader is. Who wants to try the guessing? (Choose volunteer). When you come back in take your time and wait 'til the action changes before you make a guess.

The volunteer goes out. If they are teenage or older say no peeping or cheating! If they are under ten send someone with them to cover their ears. If they are nervous and the group is large send two friends.

Now they've gone, who wants to be first leader? You can be leader. Put your hand up so everyone can see who to copy. You start us off and remember to change the action as soon as everyone's copying you.

As soon as the first action has started call in the guesser. When s/he has found the leader you can send the leader to be the next guesser. In this way the game is not held up by volunteer-hunting every few minutes. After two or three games move on to the next part of the session.

Aim *Before we go any further, I don't know everybody so let's learn a few names and then we can get on with the session.*

Shape *We need a circle for this game so let's just stand up where we are now.*

Set up *Before we start we need to know a few names so, starting with me and going round to the right, say your name slowly and clearly. Try to remember one or two of the names as we go round.*

If you look at each person as they speak and also look as if you are trying to remember the names it helps the others to do the same.

Check	*I'll never remember all those names. Let's go round once more, slowly and clearly.*

When the names have all been repeated pick up a football or some other object which can safely be thrown around the circle.

Set up	*Let's see if the circle is too big or too small for throwing this around. Just throw it from person to person and concentrate on throwing it carefully so that the other person can catch it easily.* (Short practice)
Rules	*Now for the difficult bit. From now on, when you throw the ball to someone you must say their name first. If you get the name wrong the catcher will correct you before throwing the ball to the next person.*

Throw the ball to someone whose name you remember to start the game. Keep an eye out for people who remain unnamed after a few minutes and ask those who have not yet had the ball to put up their hands. The others must then try to name them. After a short time move on to something else, even though you may not know all the names. It is better to stop before people become bored. You can always play again another day. If it is important that players should know each others' names by the end of the first session then use other name games in addition to this.

A STUDENT DIARY

As part of a course that I ran for student actors and directors the students were required to keep a diary of each class. I suggested that they devise some form of notation which would enable them to recall the games for use in their future work.

As this section of *Playing the Game* is intended for students I have included an extract from the final diary of one of my students. I am grateful to him for allowing me to reproduce it.

Introduction

The intention of the weekly classes is really to encourage and develop an awareness of the importance of the structuring of any drama workshop – the relevance of game playing; the divisions between types of games and their application within the context of a carefully devised programme of work – the needs of particular groups and individuals and the sensitivity required of the group leader to be continually taking the temperature, adapting and responding in a positive way to those needs.

What has become apparent to me over the weeks is the powerful potential of the workshop situation, not just in terms of moving towards actor training and directorial use (i.e. within the theatrical 'scene') but the sociological aspects of personal and social development of the individual in the broadest sense possible – not simply in an educational direction, although obviously the opportunities here are great, but in human interaction and 'awareness of self'.

During the term we have both played and discussed many games, exploring the considerations and difficulties attached to the setting up of the game; the placing of the game in the workshop; the purposes and aims (hidden objectives) undertaken in playing – the particular areas of development: communication, trust, sensitivity, movement, imagination, contact, group relations, confidence-building, concentration and so on.

The prime motive for using the medium of the game as a vehicle to focus on these areas lies in returning to a basic learning level which actually requires no great intellectual and inhibited adult approach. Social barriers of age and sex and 'class' rapidly crumble when adults are put into the children's world of play. It is also a world with which they are all familiar. In one way turning to games, then, is a step 'back' but in actuality the potential of that step is tremendous.

I've tried to tabulate the games attempted giving brief explanations of the setting up of the game, its aims and any problems encountered with comments at the end. Inevitably any workshop leader must compromise. There are a number of factors which may affect his original planning, not least

   i) Space   – a sports hall, classroom, W.I. hall, Drama Studio. Modification of warm-up games especially is particularly necessary in a limited space. Running around in a large space may not always be possible.

   ii) People – Every group contains different individuals!

They may be all extroverts except one or vice versa. They could be old age pensioners, infants, teenagers or kids on parole, librarians or illiterates. Responding to the needs of the individual and (if necessary) suppressing (not negatively) the outspoken or bolshy individual to allow everyone else a chance.

iii) Time – How much do you have? Will school bells interrupt every twenty minutes? What has happened before and after etc.

The content of the workshop, whether props or materials or costumes will be needed and the overall aim of the session need careful planning.

11th October N.B. Low focus/High focus – the degree of exposing the attention of the group on one individual alone.

* partner games difficult with odd numbered group.

Game – setting up	Aims	Problems/observations
KNEEFIGHTS – partners. Stand up. Hands on knees; Aim to touch partner's knees; (first to five).	Warm-up (concentration).	Useful in a limited space – great release of energy. Competitive but not consciously so. A halt called usually before anyone has called five anyway! Low focus (partners).
SWORD FIGHTS – partners, op. one hand behind back, other a finger sword. Aim to touch partner in small of back.		
GUESS THE RHYTHM. Circle. Volunteer leaves	Concentration/ movement co-ordination skills.	Volunteered 'high focus'. Necessary for the leader to

21

Game – setting up	Aims	Problems/observations
room. Volunteer leader begins rhythmic movement, repeated + followed by others. Leaver must then return to centre circle and guess leader.		keep changing the rhythm. Group co-operation i.e. not looking directly at leader.
BALL THROWING NAME GAME. Circle. Each say name – listening to others. Ball thrown, thrower saying name of catcher. If wrong, ball returned to thrower: 'I'm not x I'm y' rpt.	Getting to know; group development; co-ordination; communication.	Some experience anxiety when balls are called into play. Names are soon picked up by listeners as well as throwers. Passing high focus.
CHANGE THREE THINGS – partners: A/B; A takes a pose; B observes then closes eyes; A changes three things, e.g. hair & clothes then re-adopts pose; B guesses what's changed; reverse roles, repeat.	Concentration; memory; body control; observation; communication!	Low focus; some pairs finish earlier than others.

The progression of the class was really through release of energy to directed energy to concentration of attention to human interaction.

The notation used in the above diary is clearly intended to remind the student of the game, not to provide clear instructions for someone new to it. I find it invaluable to jot down new games or variations which I might have developed in a rehearsal or class. In this way one's store of available material is always growing. The games in this book are only some of many collected over the years.

1 WARM-UP GAMES

The games in this section are for use at the beginning of any session when the group is preparing for the work ahead. Some players need to be energized physically, others mentally. Some need to concentrate, others to relax. Common to all sessions is the need for the players to concentrate on the actual situation, that is on the space, the group and the available time.

Most players take a while to focus their concentration and energy. Warm-up games assist this process by arousing missing energy, using up spare energy, stimulating group consciousness and engaging the players' sense of fun and playfulness, both of which are essential to gaining optimum results in the later work.

The session leader can choose a game which, despite not being a serious part of the session, can utilize and develop skills needed in the work that is to follow:

a) A session of Encounter work or work requiring physical contact could start with HAPPY FAMILIES, LIVE WIRE, COLOSSUS TAG, CIRCLE CHASE or ARMS THROUGH.

b) A session that is going to demand that each player concentrates on one activity whilst others take place could start with DISTRACTIONS, MACHINES or QUICK FEELINGS.

c) QUICK FEELINGS is also a good start to a session of improvisation or performance, as is CROSS THE CIRCLE, APPLAUSE or STRINGS.

d) A session demanding teamwork can be prepared for with games such as OVER UNDER, QUEENIO or CONDUCTOR.

e) A session requiring movement control, listening or watching can start with GRANNY'S FOOTSTEPS or PUPPET STRINGS.

Games from other sections can also serve as warm-ups: A rehearsal can be started with the word game NEXT LINE? a quick and enjoyable way of testing lines. SPOT THE DIFFERENCE or PICTURE BOOK can preface a mime class.

Whatever the game, the practice of using the first few minutes as a warm-up can ensure that no-one is left behind as the work progresses. No-one will have missed vital points by having failed to concentrate fully on first entering the room.

Games included in this section

101 – Alley Cats
102 – Applause
103 – Arms Through
104 – Backs
105 – Circle Chase
106 – Colossus Tag
107 – Conductor
108 – Cross the Circle
109 – Distractions
110 – Fruit Bowl
111 – Granny's Footsteps
112 – Happy Families
113 – Knee Fights
114 – Live Wire
115 – Look Up, Look Down
116 – Machines
117 – Over Under
118 – Puppet Strings
119 – Queenio
120 – Quick Feelings
121 – Strings
122 – What's the Time Mr Wolf?

Warm-up games classified under more precise headings

RUN AROUND

101 – Alley Cats
104 – Backs
105 – Circle Chase
106 – Colossus Tag
110 – Fruit Bowl
112 – Happy Families
113 – Knee Fights
122 – What's the Time Mr Wolf?

VOCAL RELEASE

102 – Applause
107 – Conductor
109 – Distractions
112 – Happy Families

116 – Machines
120 – Quick Feelings

CO-ORDINATION AND CONTROL

103 – Arms Through
108 – Cross the Circle
111 – Granny's Footsteps
114 – Live Wire
115 – Look Up, Look Down
116 – Machines
117 – Over Under
118 – Puppet Strings
119 – Queenio
121 – Strings

101 Alley Cats

				FOCUS	– SHARED HIGH
XX					
X	X	X	X	SHAPE	– ROWS PLUS TWO
X	X	X	X	TIME	– 4–8 MINUTES
X	X	X	X	ENERGY	– HIGH
X	X	X	X	SHOW	– NO
X	X	X	X	EXTRAS	– NONE

1. Two players are chosen, one to be the cat the other to be the mouse.
2. The other players stand in rows of equal numbers.
3. There must be enough space to left and right, front and back of each player for the cat and mouse to run through the gaps.
4. The players in the rows form a series of passages by lifting their arms and so closing the gaps to their left and right. This forms passages that run from side to side.
5. At a signal from the session leader the players turn to their right, arms still lifted, which will form passages that run from front to back.
6. At the next signal they turn to face front and so on.
7. The cat now chases the mouse up and down the passages.
8. The session leader can change the direction of the passages at any time.
9. If the cat catches the mouse they reverse roles.
10. After a couple of minutes another pair are chosen to take over as cat and mouse.

102 Applause

```
        X
    X           X
    X           X
  X     X       X
  X             X
    X           X
      X       X
        X
```

FOCUS – PASSING
             VOLUNTEER HIGH
SHAPE – CIRCLE
TIME – 1–2 MINUTES
ENERGY – HIGH
SHOW – NO
EXTRAS – NONE

1. Everyone stands in a circle.
2. One by one volunteers go into the circle.
3. Each volunteer does or says something that lasts for about five seconds.
4. The rest of the group applaud wildly, whatever the volunteer has done.
5. The volunteer rejoins the circle.
6. Another volunteer runs in and so the game continues.

APPLAUSE

103 Arms Through

	XX XX	FOCUS	– LOW
XX		SHAPE	– PARTNERS
	XX	TIME	– 5–10 MINUTES
XX		ENERGY	– MEDIUM
XX	XX	SHOW	– POSSIBLE
		EXTRAS	– NONE

1. Everyone finds a partner, one is *A* and other *B*.
2. *A* stands with arms behind back, hands together.
3. *B* stands behind *A* with arms through *A's* arms, hands in front of *A*.
4. Each pair practise with *A* doing the talking and *B* being the arms. *B* can scratch *A's* head, wave at other players and so on.
5. When *A* and *B* are ready they can meet other pairs.
6. After a few minutes swap roles and go through the same sequence.

104 Backs

```
        X
    X           X       FOCUS  – LOW
    X           X       SHAPE  – CIRCLE
    X               X   TIME   – 1–2 MINUTES
    X               X   ENERGY – HIGH
    X           X       SHOW   – NO
      X         X       EXTRAS – NONE
        X
```

1. Everyone walks round the room in a circle.
2. The session leader tells them to keep as close as possible to the player in front, without distorting or decreasing the circle. This will speed up the movement, maybe to a run.
3. When the session leader calls 'Backs' all the players must try to touch the back of the person in front of them, whilst trying to keep out of range of the one behind.

105 Circle Chase

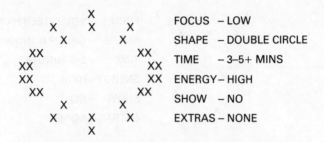

FOCUS   – LOW

SHAPE   – DOUBLE CIRCLE

TIME   – 3–5+ MINS

ENERGY – HIGH

SHOW   – NO

EXTRAS – NONE

1. Everyone finds a partner, one is *A*, the other *B*.
2. All the *A*s form a large circle, with enough space between each of them for a player to run easily through the gaps.
3. All the *B*s stand behind their partners, forming a double circle of players.
4. One pair are taken out and begin a chase, *A* chasing *B*.
5. If the person being chased, in this case *B*, stands at the front of one of the other pairs s/he is 'safe' and the person at the back of that pair becomes the one being chased.
6. If the chaser catches the chased the roles reverse immediately.

106 Colossus Tag

```
X                  X        FOCUS   – VOLUNTEER HIGH
     X    X    X            SHAPE   – GROUP RUNNING
                   X        TIME    – 3–5 MINUTES
     X    X    X            ENERGY – HIGH
                X           SHOW    – NO
          X                 EXTRAS – NONE
             X
```

1. One person is the Catcher.
2. The Catcher runs after the other players, trying to touch them.
3. The other players try not to be touched.
4. If the Catcher touches a player that player must stand still, legs astride like a Colossus, until s/he is freed.
5. A Colossus can be freed when another player crawls between their legs. A player crouched below a Colossus cannot be touched by the Catcher.
6. Once freed a player can rejoin the game.
7. A new Catcher should be chosen after a couple of minutes.

107 Conductor

```
        X
    X       X       FOCUS   – LOW
      X       X     SHAPE   – CIRCLE
    X           X   TIME    – 3–5 MINUTES
    X     X         ENERGY – HIGH
    X           X
      X       X     SHOW    – NO
              X     EXTRAS – NONE
        X
```

1. Group sits in a circle, the session leader in the centre as Conductor.
2. The group choose some situation that needs sound effects such as a band, busy street, market.
3. Different sections of the circle are given different sounds to practise; a sound that belongs to the overall picture.
4. When everyone has had a practice the Conductor starts the game.
5. When the Conductor's hand is near to the ground the sound must be very quiet, becoming louder as the Conductor's hand is raised and quieter as it is lowered.
6. A signal should be agreed for 'Stop'.
7. Choose another Conductor and try again.

108   Cross the Circle

```
            X
      X           X          FOCUS  – SHARED HIGH
      X           X          SHAPE  – CIRCLE
    X               X        TIME   – 3–5 MINUTES
    X               X        ENERGY – MEDIUM
      X           X          SHOW   – POSSIBLE
        X       X            EXTRAS – NONE
            X
```

1. Everyone sits in a circle.
2. The session leader gives each player a number: 1, 2 or 3.
3. All the number ones stand up.
4. All the number ones must cross the circle and sit down on the other side.
5. Whilst crossing the circle each player has to act as though moving through a particular environment, chosen by the session leader, for example a high wire in the circus, the moon, etc.
6. Number twos and then number threes are given different environments to try.

109 Distractions

XX		XX	FOCUS – LOW
	XX	XX	XX	SHAPE – PARTNERS
		XX	TIME – 4–5 MINUTES
	XX		ENERGY – MEDIUM
			SHOW – POSSIBLE
			EXTRAS – NONE

1. Everyone stands with a partner, one is *A*, one is *B*.
2. *A* is given a task that requires concentration, such as counting backwards from 100 to 1.
3. *B* has to distract *A*, causing a break in concentration.
4. *A* must try not to work with closed eyes.
5. *B* must not touch *A*.
6. Reverse roles.

DISTRACTIONS

35

110   Fruit Bowl

```
            X
       X              X        FOCUS  – LOW/PASSING HIGH
       X              X        SHAPE  – CIRCLE
       X        X     X        TIME   – 3–5 MINUTES
       X              X        ENERGY – HIGH
       X              X        SHOW   – NO
          X           X        EXTRAS – CHAIRS (if available)
            X
```

1. Form a circle sitting on chairs or standing.
2. The session leader gives each player the name of a fruit: apple, orange or banana.
3. One player, A, stands in the middle of the circle.
4. There is no chair/space for A in the circle.
5. A calls out the name of one type of fruit.
6. All the players who have been given the name of that fruit must change places with each other. No player may return to the seat vacated in that turn.
7. A tries to occupy one of the vacated chairs/spaces.
8. This leaves another player in the centre who becomes the next caller.
9. If the caller shouts 'Fruit Bowl' all players must change places.

111   Granny's Footsteps

```
X
X
X
X                X
X
X
X
```

FOCUS – VOLUNTEER HIGH
SHAPE – GROUP PLUS ONE
TIME   – 3–5 MINUTES
ENERGY – MEDIUM
SHOW   – POSSIBLE
EXTRAS – NONE

1. One player, *A*, stands at one end of the room, facing the wall.
2. The other players stand in a line at the opposite end of the room.
3. When the session leader calls 'Go' the players move towards *A*.
4. The first player to touch *A* on the back is the winner.
5. *A* can turn round at any point in the game and if s/he sees any player moving s/he can send them back to the beginning.
6. When *A* turns round everyone freezes.
7. The winner becomes the next *A*.

GRANNY'S FOOTSTEPS

112 Happy Families

X X	FOCUS	– LOW
X	SHAPE	– GROUP MOVING
X	TIME	– 5–8 MINUTES
X X X	ENERGY	– HIGH
X	SHOW	– NO
X X	EXTRAS	– PREPARED FAMILY CARDS

1. Form groups of three.
2. Each group of three is given the cards for one family group.
3. Each player takes one card from the family pack.
4. When the session leader shouts 'Go' all players swap cards with other players in the room as quickly and as often as possible.
5. When the session leader shouts 'Happy Families' players imitate the animals on the cards they now hold.
6. Each animal family must get together and sit on the floor, baby sitting on Mum sitting on Dad!
7. Session Leader shouts 'Go' and the card-swapping begins again.
8. The first family to sit down each time wins that game.

Note: If the group is not divisible by three, cater for the extra one or two players by using the rule that at the end of each game the winners score a point and the incomplete family loses a point.

Family cards: Prepare cards, in 'families' of animals. Each family has three cards. Each card has the name of the family, for example MONKEY, plus either FATHER or MOTHER or BABY. If made of stiff card the cards might last for more than one session but since players tend to screw them up in their excitement, you may as well use scraps of paper.

113   Knee Fights

		FOCUS	– LOW
XX	XX		
	XX	SHAPE	– PARTNERS
XX		TIME	– ONE MINUTE
	XX	ENERGY	– HIGH
XX		SHOW	– NO
	XX	EXTRAS	– NONE

1. Everyone finds a partner and stands opposite that partner in a space in the room.
2. All players put their hands on their knees; these are guarded knees.
3. All players take their hands off their knees; these are unguarded knees.
4. When the session leader calls 'Go' everyone tries to grab their partner's knees.
5. One point is scored for every touch on an unguarded knee.
6. First person to score five is the winner.
7. Any player who keeps guarding their knees for more than thirty seconds is out.

Note: This is an excellent warm-up for all ages and all spaces, however small. It is also useful for groups who are not wearing appropriate clothes for other warm-ups in which running around is required. It does not matter if there are no winners; stop the game after a minute or less.

114 Live Wire

```
            X
    X               X       FOCUS   – PASSING HIGH
    X               X       SHAPE   – CIRCLE
    X               X       TIME    – 3–5 MINUTES
    X       X       X       ENERGY – LOW
    X               X       SHOW    – NO
        X           X       EXTRAS – NONE
            X
```

1. Everyone stands in a circle.
2. One player stands in the middle of the circle with closed eyes.
3. All the players in the circle hold hands to form an unbroken circle.
4. The session leader sends a hand-squeeze around the circle by squeezing one of the two hands s/he is holding. The hand-squeeze may be passed to left or right by the player receiving it, but each player is only allowed one squeeze per go, since to squeeze both hands causes chaos!
5. The player in the centre of the circle has to guess where the squeeze is (with open eyes).

115 Look Up, Look Down

```
        X
   X        X        FOCUS  – LOW
   X        X        SHAPE  – CIRCLE
   X        X        TIME   – 3–5 MINUTES
   X        X        ENERGY – LOW
   X        X        SHOW   – NO
     X      X        EXTRAS – NONE
        X
```

1. Everyone stands in a circle and looks at the floor.
2. When the session leader calls 'Look up' every player looks up and at another player.
3. When the session leader calls 'Look down' every player looks down at the floor.
4. If two players make eye contact when 'Look up' is called, they are both out and must sit down.
5. The winner is the last player left standing.

Note: This should be a fast-moving game.

116 Machines

```
            X
        X       X        FOCUS  – PASSING/SHARED
      X           X      SHAPE  – CIRCLE
    X               X    TIME   – 3–8 MINUTES
    X               X    ENERGY – MEDIUM
      X           X      SHOW   – POSSIBLE
        X       X        EXTRAS – NONE
            X
```

1. Everyone stands in a circle.
2. One player goes in to the centre of the circle and begins the game with a movement and sound which s/he keeps repeating until the whole machine is complete.
3. A second player joins the machine with a movement and sound which complements that being made by the first player.
4. One by one the rest of the group quickly join in until the machine is complete.

Note: This game can also be played in groups with each group being allowed time to prepare a machine which is then shown to the other players. If appropriate, signals can be devised which instruct the machine to go faster, slower or to stop.

117 Over Under

X	X	X		
X	X	X	FOCUS	– LOW
X	X	X	SHAPE	– TEAMS
X	X	X	TIME	– 3–8 MINUTES
X	X	X	ENERGY	– HIGH
X	X	X	SHOW	– NO
X	X	X	EXTRAS	– 1 BALL PER TEAM
X	X	X		

1. Split the group into teams of equal numbers.
2. One player from each team is given a football.
3. The players with footballs stand at the front of the room, their teams lined up behind them.
4. When the session leader calls 'Go' the front players pass the footballs over their heads to the next in line.
5. The second players pass the footballs through their legs to the next in line, who pass them over their heads.
6. The football is passed from player to player in this way until it reaches the last player in the line, who runs to the front and begins the next sequence with an overhead pass.
7. When the original front player is once more at the front of the team the team sits down.
8. The first team to sit down wins the game.

Note: If there are no footballs, the players can play by jumping over and crawling under each other.

118   Puppet Strings

```
XX
        XX              FOCUS  – LOW
  XX          XX        SHAPE  – PARTNERS
        XX              TIME   – 5–10 MINUTES
  XX                    ENERGY – LOW
              XX        SHOW   – POSSIBLE
    XX                  EXTRAS – NONE
```

1. Everyone finds a partner – one is *A*, the other *B*.
2. *A* is the puppeteer and stands opposite *B* who is to be the puppet on a string.
3. *A* moves *B* without touching *B*.
4. *A* indicates the part of the body which s/he wishes *B* to move by tapping it.
5. *A* then pulls on an imaginary string and *B* responds as if the string went up over a bar and down to the part of *B*'s body already indicated by *A*.
6. All the time that *A* pulls the string *B* responds by raising the appropriate part of the body.
7. When *A* puts up a hand to indicate 'Stop' *B* holds that position.
8. Swap roles.

Note: It is possible to get the puppets to walk – try it!

119 Queenio

```
X
X                         FOCUS   – VOLUNTEER HIGH
X                         SHAPE   – LINE PLUS ONE
X                    X
X                         TIME    – 3–8 MINUTES
X                         ENERGY – MEDIUM
X                         SHOW    – NO
X
X                         EXTRAS  – TENNIS BALL
```

1. One player, *A*, is given a tennis ball.
2. The other players stand side by side, as close to each other as possible, in a line behind *A*, hands behind backs.
3. Without looking, *A* throws the ball towards the line.
4. One of the players in the line picks up the ball and it is concealed somewhere along the line.
5. The line now calls in unison: 'Queenio Queenio who's got the ballio?'
6. *A* turns round to face the line and tries to guess who is concealing the ball.
7. *A* can ask up to three players at a time to move about, with instructions such as 'Put out your hands; turn around; jump up and down' and so on.
8. The players in the line can pass the ball along, making sure that *A* does not notice them do so.
9. *A* may not touch any of the other players.

Note: If no tennis ball is available any small object will do, preferably one which would not break if dropped.

Rehearsal note: With ticklish players this game works wonders as a way of provoking someone into denouncing friends! In absence of a tennis ball I once used a pingpong ball instead which being so small was much more easily concealed by the players. This was part of the warm-up for a rehearsal of a witch-hunting scene in which a girl denounces her friend after suffering at the hands of the witch-hunter's assistant, a dab hand with needles when looking for 'the devil's mark'. The actual pricking scene was very short and it had been difficult for the student actress to be convinced that such a change of loyalties was possible . . . until we played Queenio.

I had two Queenios instead of one, the witch-hunter and his assistant. I also abandoned the no-touching rule – they *had* to find that pingpong ball. I allowed them to call players out of the line to be questioned and searched, a new line being formed by those thought not to have the ball. I did not tell the players that this was a character exercise, though I had deliberately arranged the game in such a way that the groupings in the play were being strengthened. What transpired was a bonus for us all.

The actress playing the girl in the pricking scene was very ticklish. The two searchers did not tickle her deliberately, nor were they intending her any harm. They were behaving in a very functional and unemotional way and were determined to find the ball. The girl went to pieces as soon as she began to feel tickled. She pulled herself down onto the floor and began to assure them that she did not have the ball and that they must stop because she couldn't stand being tickled. This quickly became a cry of 'If you won't believe me I'll tell you who's got it but please let me go!' The whole thing had taken less than twenty seconds. The actress had surprised herself and said to me afterwards 'I would have done anything to stop them.'

120 Quick Feelings

```
        X
  X           X        FOCUS   – LOW
   X          X        SHAPE   – CIRCLE
 X              X      TIME    – 3–5 MINUTES
 X              X      ENERGY – HIGH
  X           X        SHOW    – POSSIBLE
   X          X        EXTRAS – NONE
        X
```

1. Mark out a large cross on the floor (with chalk, shoes, chairs, etc.).
2. Choose four feelings, such as ANGRY, HAPPY, SAD and FRIGHTENED. Each section formed by the cross represents one of the feelings and should be marked accordingly (with chalk, coloured paper etc.).
3. The players walk in a circle around the cross.
4. At a given signal from the session leader all the players stop.
5. When the players stop they must act immediately as if their feelings were those indicated, each player responding to the one in the section s/he has stopped in.
6. No player may leave a section until the session leader signals that they may walk round again.
7. In the ANGRY section no player may touch another player!

Note: You can vary the game by indicating different categories in the sections, such as jobs, ages, times of day and so on.

Rehearsal note: The game can be played by actors in role: when a character stops in one of the sections s/he voices the points in the play which arouse such feelings for the character.

QUICK FEELINGS

121 Strings

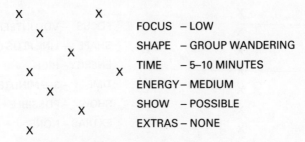

X   X
 X
   X
X   X
 X
    X
 X

FOCUS – LOW
SHAPE – GROUP WANDERING
TIME   – 5–10 MINUTES
ENERGY – MEDIUM
SHOW   – POSSIBLE
EXTRAS – NONE

1. The players walk around the room.
2. The session leader asks them to imagine that there are strings attached to various points of their bodies. At any one time they are being pulled by only one of these strings.
3. The session leader calls out a part of the body and the players move as if led by that part.
4. The players experiment using fast and slow walks and discuss the type of person suggested by each.

Rehearsal note: Good lead in to work on comic figures or caricatures.

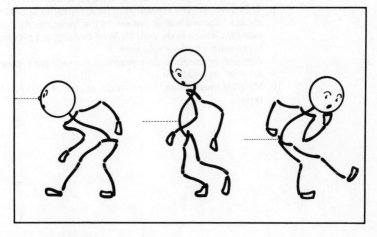

STRINGS

49

122   What's the Time Mr Wolf?

```
X
X                           FOCUS  – VOLUNTEER HIGH
X              X            SHAPE  – LINE PLUS ONE
X                           ENERGY– HIGH
X                           TIME   – 3–5 MINUTES
X                           SHOW   – POSSIBLE
X                           EXTRAS – NONE
X
```

1. One person is the catcher, Mr Wolf.
2. Mr Wolf stands at one end of the room, facing the wall.
3. The other players have a safe area marked out at the other end of the room in which they wait.
4. As soon as Mr Wolf turns to face the other players they must leave their area.
5. They can only return to the safe area if chased by Mr Wolf.
6. As they leave their area the players chant 'What's the time Mr Wolf?'
7. Mr Wolf chooses a time of day and replies ' . . . o'clock' as s/he begins to pace up and down beside the wall.
8. This question and answer routine is repeated until Mr Wolf shouts 'dinner-time' in answer to the question. At this point the chase is on with Mr Wolf chasing the players who try to return to their safe area.
9. Any player caught before reaching the safe area must join Mr Wolf as a catcher.
10. Mr Wolf must shout 'dinner-time' as one of the first six replies.

2 OBSERVATION GAMES

It has been said that observation is the key to creativity; if you notice nothing you have little to say.

The games in this section are intended to develop the players' awareness of the world around them, not by pointing out that world to them but rather by developing their own ability to see, hear and concentrate.

Some of the games involve spotting verbal or visual clues, some involve presenting such clues to the rest of the group.

Observation can provide material for stories and improvisation, therefore games from this section can be used as a preparation for such work. Warm-up games can be used to prepare players for the observation games:

a) For listening games prepare with GRANNY'S FOOTSTEPS so that the players are used to moving quietly.

b) For watching games prepare with LOOK UP, LOOK DOWN, PUPPET STRINGS or CONDUCTOR.

c) For concentration games prepare with ALLEY CATS or DISTRACTIONS.

d) For physical control try OVER UNDER, QUEENIO or MACHINES.

Games included in this section

201 – Alibi
202 – Blind Pictures
203 – Blind Tag
204 – Chinese Mime
205 – Echoes
206 – Eye for a Tooth
207 – Find the Line
208 – Fizz Buzz
209 – Guess the Leader
210 – In the Manner of the Word
211 – Lateral Codes
212 – Lost Chord
213 – Me to You
214 – Memory Object
215 – Mirrors
216 – Morse Code
217 – Pirate's Gold
218 – Red Ball, Yellow Ball
219 – Sound Pictures
220 – Spot the Difference
221 – Ventriloquist
222 – Whizz! Zoom!
223 – Wink Murder
224 – Yes, No

Observation games classified under more precise headings

LISTENING

201 – Alibi
202 – Blind Pictures
203 – Blind Tag
205 – Echoes
207 – Find the Line
208 – Fizz Buzz
209 – Guess the Leader
211 – Lateral Codes
212 – Lost Chord
213 – Me to You
216 – Morse Code
217 – Pirate's Gold
219 – Sound Pictures

222 – Whizz! Zoom!
224 – Yes, No

LOOKING

204 – Chinese Mime
206 – Eye for a Tooth
209 – Guess the Leader
210 – In the Manner of the Word
211 – Lateral Codes
214 – Memory Object
215 – Mirrors
218 – Red Ball, Yellow Ball
220 – Spot the Difference
223 – Wink Murder

CO-ORDINATION AND CONTROL

202 – Blind Pictures
203 – Blind Tag
204 – Chinese Mime
206 – Eye for a Tooth
207 – Find the Line
209 – Guess the Leader
210 – In the Manner of the Word
212 – Lost Chord
213 – Me to You
215 – Mirrors
217 – Pirate's Gold
218 – Red Ball, Yellow Ball
220 – Spot the Difference
221 – Ventriloquist
222 – Whizz! Zoom!
223 – Wink Murder

201 Alibi

```
        X
    X           X       FOCUS   – VOLUNTEER HIGH
    X               X   SHAPE   – CIRCLE
  X               X     TIME    – 5–15 MINUTES
  X         X       X   ENERGY – LOW
  X               X     SHOW    – NO
    X             X     EXTRAS – NONE
      X     X
        X
```

1. Everyone sits in a circle.
2. A volunteer goes into the centre of the circle and plays the role of detective.
3. Each player in the circle must answer any question asked by the detective as if they are all playing the same person, the chief suspect.
4. A crime is agreed as the subject for the investigation.
5. The detective asks questions of the group as if they were the chief suspect. S/he is trying to break their alibi.
6. If any player contradicts something said earlier s/he is out and the detective has won. For example, if the detective asks for the suspect's name and is told 'John Paul Robson' but later, in answer to the same question another player says 'Paul Robinson' then the detective wins.

Note: Advise the detective to repeat questions some time into the 'case' as this is the only way to encourage contradiction from the suspect.

202   Blind Pictures

```
X   X  X   X
X  X   X
X  X
X                           X
              X   X      FOCUS   – SHARED
          X   X          SHAPE   – TEAMS
        X   X   X        TIME    – 10–15 MINUTES
      X  X   X  X        ENERGY – MEDIUM
                         SHOW    – POSSIBLE
                         EXTRAS – NONE
```

FOCUS   – SHARED
SHAPE   – TEAMS
TIME   – 10–15 MINUTES
ENERGY – MEDIUM
SHOW   – POSSIBLE
EXTRAS – NONE

1. Split the group into two teams, *A* and *B*.
2. Team *A* stands with eyes closed.
3. Team *B* arranges team *A* into a 'statue picture' of some well-known event or situation such as Noah's Ark or a football match.
4. Team *B* must not give any verbal clues to the picture.
5. Team *A* tries to guess the picture without opening its eyes.
6. Each member of team *A* describes the position s/he is in and from this they try to guess the picture.
7. When team *A* has guessed the players open their eyes to see the picture.
8. Team *A* then arranges team *B* into a blind picture.

203 Blind Tag

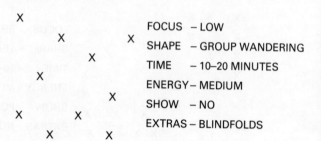

FOCUS – LOW
SHAPE – GROUP WANDERING
TIME – 10–20 MINUTES
ENERGY – MEDIUM
SHOW – NO
EXTRAS – BLINDFOLDS

1. Each player wears a blindfold (or closes eyes).
2. One player is given a set of keys. Whoever holds the keys is the Hunter.
3. The Hunter tries to give the keys to one of the other players, if s/he can find one.
4. The other players try to avoid the Hunter and the keys.
5. Whenever the Hunter moves s/he must shake the keys but when s/he is still s/he can be silent.
6. If the Hunter touches another player that player must take the keys and become the new Hunter.
7. The new Hunter must wait ten seconds before beginning to move.

Development:

8. Choose a safe area where the Hunter may not go.
9. Throw a football amongst the players.
10. If a player can pick up the football and get to the safe area with it s/he may remove the blindfold and throw the football back into the group.

Note: If this is the first blindfold game in the session allow at least twenty minutes for it so that the players have time to explore the space with their blindfolds on before being hunted. I also take at least three players out of the game for a few minutes at a time, to help me keep an eye out for players bumping into things around the room.

204 Chinese Mime

```
X   X   X    X   X   X
  X   X X   X X   X X
      X              (XXXX)
```

FOCUS   – PASSING
          HIGH

SHAPE   – GROUP
          WATCH ONE

TIME   – 10–20
          MINUTES

ENERGY – MEDIUM

SHOW   – YES

EXTRAS – NONE

1. Five volunteers are chosen.
2. Four of the volunteers leave the room; one remains.
3. The audience suggest a simple event which the volunteer, number one, is to mime. For example, 'You are fishing; something pulls the line; it's not a fish it's a bicycle wheel; you pack up and roll the wheel home.'
4. The four volunteers are now recalled into the room and given numbers: two, three, four and five.
5. Numbers three, four and five sit with their backs to the audience.
6. Numbers one and two stand in the area between the two groups.
7. Number two watches number one perform the mime.
8. Number one joins the audience and number three is called to watch number two repeat the mime.
9. This sequence is repeated with numbers four and five.
10. Number five does not perform the mime, instead s/he offers a suggestion as to what it might represent.
11. Before the audience offer the correct storyline, numbers four, three and two offer their impressions.

205 Echoes

```
        XX              XX
            XX                    FOCUS   – LOW
        XX                        SHAPE   – PARTNERS
                                  TIME    – 5 MINUTES
                XX                ENERGY – MEDIUM
        XX              XX        SHOW    – NO
                        XX        EXTRAS – BLINDFOLDS
            XX
```

1. Everyone finds a partner, one is *A* the other *B*.
2. Each pair agree a sound between them which will be their call to each other.
3. All the pairs demonstrate their calls to ensure that no two are the same. (If they are, change one.)
4. The players scatter around the room, *A* being as far as possible away from *B*.
5. The players put on blindfolds.
6. At a signal from the session leader all the players begin to make their call, listening for that of their partner.
7. When a pair find each other they may take off their blindfolds and watch the others, silently.

Note: In absence of blindfolds players can close their eyes.

206 Eye for a Tooth

```
        X
   X         X        FOCUS  – VOLUNTEER HIGH
  X              X    SHAPE  – CIRCLE
 X                X   TIME   – 3–5 MINUTES
 X       X
 X               X    ENERGY – LOW
   X             X    SHOW   – NO
     X         X      EXTRAS – NONE
        X
```

1. The players sit in a circle.
2. One player, *A*, sits in the centre of the circle.
3. *A* looks at one of the other players and does two things: (*i*) S/he names a part of the body using the phrase 'This is my . . . (e.g. nose).' *ii*) At the same time s/he points to a part of the body which may or may not be the same as that mentioned.
4. If *A* points to the part s/he has named the player spoken to gives one handclap.
5. If *A* points to a part different from that which s/he named the other player must point to the part named and name the part pointed at.
6. Any player who goes wrong is out. (In a large group it saves the boredom of those who are out to change the penalty to taking over in the centre of the circle.)
7. Speed it up.

207 Find the Line

```
X     X     X
X     X     X     FOCUS  – LOW
X     X     X     SHAPE  – TEAMS
X     X     X     TIME    – 5–10 MINUTES
X     X     X     ENERGY – MEDIUM
X     X     X     SHOW   – NO
X     X     X     EXTRAS – BLINDFOLDS
```

1. Split the group into teams.
2. A line is drawn or marked in some way on the floor.
3. One player from each team, A, stands on the line.
4. The other players stand in a line, one behind the other, each team behind its respective A.
5. All players choose a sound which is to be the call by which the rest of the team recognize them.
6. All players learn the call of the person in front of them. (A does not have one to learn.)
7. The players scatter around the room.
8. Each player puts on a blindfold.
9. At a signal from the session leader the teams have to regroup in the same order as before with A standing on the marked line.
10. The session leader stands at one end of the line throughout the search saying 'Line here.'
11. When a team has regrouped they can remove their blindfolds and watch the others, silently.

Note: In absence of blindfolds the players may close their eyes.

208 Fizz Buzz

```
        X
   X         X        FOCUS   – PASSING HIGH
   X         X        SHAPE   – CIRCLE
  X            X      TIME    – 3–8 MINUTES
  X            X      ENERGY – LOW
   X         X        SHOW    – NO
    X       X         EXTRAS – NONE
        X
```

1. The players sit in a circle.
2. One player, A, calls out 'one.'
3. The player to the right of A calls out 'two'.
4. This continues round and round until a player reaches 'thirty-five'.
5. There are two rules: *i*) On every multiple of *five* the number is not called out. Instead the player calls 'Fizz'. *ii*) On every multiple of *seven* the number is not called out. Instead the player calls 'Buzz'.
6. The number *thirty-five* therefore becomes 'Fizz Buzz'.
7. Introduce the rules one at a time and practise each before trying Fizz Buzz.

Note: This is a team game, the aim being to get to Fizz Buzz successfully.

209 Guess the Leader

		FOCUS	– SHARED HIGH
		SHAPE	– CIRCLE
		TIME	– 5–10 MINUTES
		ENERGY	– MEDIUM
		SHOW	– NO
		EXTRAS	– NONE

1. The players sit in a circle.
2. The session leader announces that s/he is about to test the players' quick responses. They must copy the action s/he is about to start. At any time s/he may change the action and they must pick up the change as quickly as they can.
3. The session leader begins with a handclap and every fifteen seconds or so s/he changes the action.
4. After about six changes s/he stops and announces that the game involves a player guessing who the leader is.
5. One player, *A*, volunteers to be the guesser and leaves the room whilst the rest of the group choose a new leader, *B*.
6. Once *B* has established the first action, *A* is recalled and stands in the middle of the circle.
7. *A* has three guesses.
8. *B* becomes the next guesser.

Note: With a new or inexperienced group, if the session leader is having difficulty finding a volunteer to be the guesser, suggest that two friends are joint guessers.

210 In the Manner of the Word

```
        X
    X       X       FOCUS  – SHARED HIGH
    X       X       SHAPE  – CIRCLE
  X         X       TIME   – 5–10 MINUTES
  X       X         ENERGY – MEDIUM
    X       X       SHOW   – YES
    X       X       EXTRAS – NONE
        X
```

1. The players sit in a circle.
2. One player, A, leaves the room.
3. The other players choose an adverb. (Explain it as 'the sort of word that describes how you can do things, like happily, nervously or suspiciously'.)
4. When everyone is sure what word has been chosen A is recalled.
5. A chooses four or five players who stand up.
6. A asks these players to perform some imaginary task such as sweeping the road or reading a magazine.
7. The players must perform the imaginary task IN THE MANNER OF THE WORD they have chosen.
8. By watching the way in which they perform the task A tries to guess what the word is.
9. A is allowed three changes of group and/or task to help the guess.

Note: If you are interested in the debate that surrounds the choosing of the adverb you can send someone with A and tell them to make up a list of tasks between them. This prevents boredom setting in as A awaits the recall.

211 Lateral Codes

```
            X
      X           X       FOCUS  – PASSING HIGH
      X           X       SHAPE  – CIRCLE
    X               X     TIME   – 5–10 MINUTES
    X               X     ENERGY – LOW
      X           X       SHOW   – NO
        X       X         EXTRAS – PENCILS, PENS,
            X                      MATCHES
```

1. The session leader takes three volunteers aside and tells them a sequence of words and actions which they are to perform on returning to the group. The sequence operates according to a code which is explained to them.
2. The three volunteers return to the circle and each of them, in turn, performs a sequence which demonstrates the code.
3. The rest of the group try to guess what the code is.
4. Each player in the circle makes an attempt at a sequence which fits the code.
5. Any player who cracks the code is told that s/he has done so by the three volunteers and from then onwards s/he operates according to the code.

Examples of codes:

i) Some matches or pens are put on the floor. Each volunteer, in turn, picks up some of the objects and then replaces them, saying a number as the last object is replaced. The number of objects picked up can vary. Each volunteer passes a comment as s/he performs the task, natural comments such as 'Easy really', 'Got it yet?', 'You'll guess it soon', 'I'll make a pattern shall I?' and so on.
Code: The number spoken as the last object is replaced has nothing to do with the number of objects picked up. It refers to the number of words in the phrase spoken. A player who said 'Got it?' as s/he picked up the objects would say 'Two' as s/he replaced the last one; a player saying 'Easy isn't it?' would say 'Three'.

ii) The volunteers pass two matches or pens around the

circle. As a volunteer passes the objects to the next player s/he performs an elaborate or simple a routine as s/he likes which results in the objects either forming a cross or not. At the same time s/he says either 'I pass these to you crossed' or 'I pass these to you uncrossed'.

Code: The code is nothing to do with the objects. The phrase refers to whether the player's legs or feet are crossed or uncrossed when the objects are passed on.

212   Lost Chord

```
          X
    X            X        FOCUS  – LOW
    X            X        SHAPE  – CIRCLE
   X              X       TIME   – 5 MINUTES
   X              X       ENERGY – MEDIUM
    X            X        SHOW   – NO
     X           X        EXTRAS – BLINDFOLDS
          X
```

1. The players stand in a circle.
2. One by one each player makes a noise.
3. The noises must all be different and the players must remember their own noise plus those of the player to their right and left.
4. The players scatter around the room and put on blindfolds.
5. At a signal from the session leader the players start making their noises whilst listening for the calls of the players who were next to them in the circle.
6. The players try to reform the circle.

Note: In absence of blindfolds players can close their eyes.

213 Me to You

```
        X
    X        X        FOCUS  – PASSING HIGH
    X        X        SHAPE  – CIRCLE
    X            X    TIME   – 5–8 MINUTES
    X            X    ENERGY – MEDIUM
      X          X    SHOW   – NO
        X        X    EXTRAS – NONE
        X
```

1. The players sit or stand in a circle.
2. One player calls out 'One'.
3. The rest of the group number round from 'one'.
4. Players must remember their number.
5. A rhythm is set up as follows: slap right leg; slap left leg; click right fingers; click left fingers. This is continued throughout the game.
6. One starts by calling 'One to . . .', adding a number, for example 'One to seven'.
7. Number seven must now carry on by saying first 'Seven to . . .' and then the number of another player.
8. The words fit into the rhythm, each number being said on one of the two clicks.
9. Any player who makes a mistake moves and becomes the last number, standing next to One. Players adjust their numbers accordingly.
10. Each player's aim: to become One.

214 Memory Object

XX			FOCUS	– LOW
	XX		SHAPE	– PARTNERS
XX		XX	TIME	– 5–10 MINUTES
		XX	ENERGY	– LOW
	XX		SHOW	– NO
XX		XX	EXTRAS	– 1 OBJECT PER PAIR

1. Everyone finds a partner, one is *A*, the other *B*.
2. *A* is given an object and told to inspect it as carefully as possible for about thirty seconds.
3. *B* then removes and conceals the object.
4. *A* describes the object in as much detail as possible.
5. *B* returns the object to *A* and they discuss the accuracy of the description.
6. The game is then repeated with a different object being given to *B* for examination.

Note: If there are no suitable objects available the players can study their partners for thirty seconds, closing their eyes when attempting a description.

215 Mirrors

XX				
	XX		FOCUS	– LOW
XX		XX	SHAPE	– PARTNERS
		XX	TIME	– 5–10 MINUTES
XX		XX	ENERGY	– LOW
XX		XX	SHOW	– POSSIBLE
	XX		EXTRAS	– NONE

1. Everyone finds a partner, one is *A* the other *B*.
2. *A* stands facing *B*.
3. *A* begins a movement.
4. *B* copies the movement as if s/he was *A*'s mirror-image.
5. Reverse roles.

Note: After practice more definite movements can be suggested to the players such as a clown putting on makeup or someone trying on a costume.

MIRRORS

216 Morse Code

XX					FOCUS	– SHARED	
		XX			SHAPE	– PARTNERS	
	XX				TIME	– 5–10 MINUTES	
			XX		ENERGY	– MEDIUM	
	XX			XX	SHOW	– POSSIBLE	
XX		XX			EXTRAS	– NONE	

1. Everyone finds a partner, one is *A* the other *B*.
2. Each pair prepares a short rhythmic sequence that they can clap to each other.
3. After practising the rhythmic phrases the players divide into two lines, in one all the *A*s and in the other all the *B*s.
4. The *A*s sit at one end of the room in a line facing the wall.
5. The *B*s stand in a line about three paces behind the *A*s, making sure that no-one is standing behind their partner.
6. One of the *B* group claps out the rhythm s/he devised earlier.
7. If the correct *A* recognizes the phrase s/he claps it in reply.
8. If the wrong *A* responds then *B* must repeat the phrase once more.
9. When each player has had at least two attempts reverse roles, *B*s listening and *A*s clapping.

217   Pirate's Gold

```
X        X  X  X      X   FOCUS   – SHARED
X                     X   SHAPE   – GROUP + ONE
X                     X   TIME    – 5–10 MINUTES
X                     X   ENERGY – MEDIUM
              X           SHOW    – POSSIBLE
                          EXTRAS – BLINDFOLD, KEYS
```

1. One player volunteers to be the Pirate.
2. The Pirate sits or stands at one end of the room and is blindfolded.
3. A bunch of keys is placed in front of the Pirate's feet; this is the Gold.
4. The other players wait silently at the sides of the room.
5. At a signal from the session leader three players move to the end of the room opposite the Pirate.
6. When the session leader says 'Go' the three players creep up to the Pirate to steal the Gold.
7. If the Pirate hears a sound s/he points in the direction of that sound. If anyone is standing on the line indicated by the Pirate s/he is out, at which point the session leader calls 'Freeze'.
8. When 'Freeze' is called the three players must stop; the one who is out moves to the side; another player moves to the starting line; the session leader calls 'Go'; the game recommences. In this way the Pirate is not confused by the sounds of a changeover and the two remaining players cannot seize the chance of racing for the gold.

PIRATE'S GOLD

218 Red Ball, Yellow Ball

```
            X
      X           X        FOCUS   – LOW
      X                X   SHAPE   – CIRCLE
   X                   X   TIME    – 3–5 MINUTES
   X                   X   ENERGY – MEDIUM
      X                X   SHOW    – NO
         X           X     EXTRAS – TWO FOOTBALLS
            X
```

1. The players stand in a circle.
2. One football is introduced as being 'red' irrespective of what colour it actually is.
3. The other football is introduced as being 'yellow'.
4. Whenever a football is being thrown the thrower must call out 'red' or 'yellow', according to which ball it is.
5. The game begins with the 'red' ball being thrown around the circle.
6. After a minute or so the 'yellow' ball is brought into play as well.
7. The players try to keep both footballs moving without either being dropped.

Note: If a player tries to watch one football only, the other will most probably be dropped. Look straight ahead and both can be seen.

219 Sound Pictures

```
X    X
X  X    X
X    X              FOCUS   – LOW
X  X                SHAPE   – TWO TEAMS
                    TIME    – 10–20 MINUTES
               X    ENERGY – MEDIUM
     X  X    X      SHOW    – YES
     X  X    X      EXTRAS – OBJECTS
       X    X                (OPTIONAL)
```

1. The group is divided into two teams, one *A* the other *B*.
2. Team *A* lie on the floor with eyes closed.
3. Team *B* go outside and choose an environment which they can create with sounds, such as a factory, the sea and so on.
4. Team *B* then re-enter the room and try to create their chosen scene using sounds (which can be made with or without objects).
5. Team *A* then guess what the scene could have been, what the sounds reminded them of.
6. Reverse roles.

Note: If this is the first sound game of the session it may help both to spend time playing a listening game and to explore the sounds that can be made with the different surfaces/objects in the room.

220 Spot the Difference

XX	FOCUS – LOW
XX	SHAPE – PARTNERS
XX	TIME – 5–10 MINUTES
XX XX	ENERGY – LOW
XX	SHOW – POSSIBLE
XX	EXTRAS – NONE

1. Everyone finds a partner, one is *A* the other *B*.
2. *A* takes up a position and 'freezes', like a statue.
3. *B* looks carefully at *A*'s statue and tries to remember as much detail as possible.
4. *B* then turns round so that s/he cannot see *A*.
5. *A* changes three details such as moving a piece of jewellery or clothing, repositioning a foot or hand, and so on.
6. *A* calls *B* who turns round to face *A* once more.
7. *B* tries to spot which details have changed.
8. Reverse roles.

SPOT THE DIFFERENCE

221 Ventriloquist

```
        X
     X      X        FOCUS  – PASSING HIGH
     X             X  SHAPE  – CIRCLE
     X             X  TIME   – 5–10 MINUTES
            X
     X             X  ENERGY – LOW
       X           X  SHOW   – POSSIBLE
         X       X    EXTRAS – NONE
            X
```

1. The players sit in a circle.
2. One player, *A*, sits in the centre of the circle.
3. *A* questions the other players and may ask any player any question.
4. When *A* speaks to a player that player must not react in any way.
5. When *A* speaks to a player the person sitting to the *left* of that player must answer for them.
6. If the person to the left of the player being spoken to forgets to speak s/he is out.
7. If the person being spoken to speaks or moves s/he is out.
8. *A* tries to get all the players out.

222 Whizz! Zoom!

```
        X
    X       X       FOCUS   – PASSING HIGH
    X       X       SHAPE   – CIRCLE
  X           X     TIME    – 3–5 MINUTES
  X           X     ENERGY – MEDIUM
    X       X       SHOW    – NO
      X     X       EXTRAS – NONE
        X
```

1. The players sit in a circle.
2. Each player may only say two words, 'Whizz' or 'Zoom'.
3. If a player speaks to the person to the left s/he says 'Zoom'.
4. If s/he speaks to the person on the right s/he says 'Whizz'.
5. Only one player speaks at a time.
6. A player must speak only if spoken to.
7. Players may use one word per turn and may choose either of the two permitted words, turning to the appropriate listener.
8. Speed it up.

223   Wink Murder

```
          X
     X         X        FOCUS  – LOW
     X         X        SHAPE  – CIRCLE
   X             X      TIME   – 5–20 MINUTES
   X             X      ENERGY – LOW
     X         X        SHOW   – YES
      X       X         EXTRAS – NONE
          X
```

1. The players sit in a circle with closed eyes.
2. The session leader walks around the circle and touches one player on the head.
3. That player is the Killer.
4. The session leader continues around the circle and sits down.
5. The players open their eyes.
6. The Killer murders people by winking at them. S/he is trying to murder all the other players.
7. If a player sees the Killer winking s/he must silently count to ten before 'dying'. S/he may not reveal the identity of the Killer.
8. If a wink directed towards one player is spotted by another, the second player is free to comment on this to the others since only a direct wink causes 'death' and silence.
9. The players try to detect the Killer but must reach a unanimous agreement before making an accusation.
10. If a false accusation is made the Killer wins; if a correct accusation is made the Killer loses; if the Killer manages to murder all but one s/he wins.
11. The Killer may join in the debate.

224   Yes, No

```
X  X  X
   X  X                      FOCUS  – SHARED
          X                  SHAPE  – SMALL GROUPS
       X      X              TIME   – 8–15 MINUTES
          X  X               ENERGY – LOW
      X  X                   SHOW   – POSSIBLE
   X        X                EXTRAS – NONE
      X  X
```

1. Split the group into smaller groups of five or six players.
2. One player in each group, A, is questioned by the rest of the group.
3. A must not use the words 'Yes' or 'No'.
4. The other players try to make A use yes and no.
5. If A says either word s/he is out.
6. If A lasts one minute without using either word s/he has succeeded and the game moves on.
7. Every player has a turn.

3 ENCOUNTER GAMES

If individuals within a group feel comfortable in each others' company it is much easier for them to establish a good working relationship.

When the work in question is play, it becomes much more important that trust and support exist within the group as many games involve taking a risk, whether physical (blindfold games), social (games which rely on personal information), or creative (improvisation and story-making). Any game of this type can be spoilt or hindered by wariness and embarrassment.

If the games are to be more than an end in themselves, if they are being used as part of a developmental process for the individual, the group and the project in hand, then it is important to foster trust, support and encouragement within the group as soon as possible.

In the same way that the use of low focus games enables players to develop the confidence needed to volunteer for high focus situations, Encounter games are designed to assist this process, being specifically concerned with developing trust and support.

Most of the games in this section involve physical contact either as the main aspect, as in I KNOW THAT HAND, or as an essential but unnoticed aspect, as in TRUST CIRCLE.

Some of the games involve the sharing of personal details ranging from the basic and essential detail of name (hence the three name games), to habits (SILLY ME).

Although physical contact and talking about oneself can help to build trust and support within a group, the group leader must be careful not to exploit the readiness with which some people will divulge personal secrets or develop physical contact when in fact they are not ready to cope with the personal implications of this. Reticent group members may be led to think that this is what is required which, since they are unable or unwilling to comply, indicates to them a personal failure.

Encounter games are used here for group development in order to facilitate the playing of creative and presentational games. In this context they are not a part of psychodrama or drama therapy and anyone wishing to develop either of these applications should seek professional advice and training before doing so.

Games included in this section

301 – Birthdays
302 – Blind Killer
303 – Blind Trust
304 – Catch the Name
305 – Guard and Thief
306 – Home Chase
307 – I Know that Hand
308 – If S/he Was a Tree
309 – In the Manner of the Person
310 – Let's All Be Me
311 – Name Chain
312 – Poker Face
313 – Silly Me
314 – Tell Me True
315 – Trust Circle
316 – Turn Round

Encounter games classified under more precise headings

INTRODUCTIONS

304 – Catch the Name
306 – Home Chase
310 – Let's All Be Me
311 – Name Chain
313 – Silly Me

PHYSICAL

302 – Blind Killer
303 – Blind Trust
304 – Catch the Name
305 – Guard and Thief
306 – Home Chase
307 – I Know that Hand
309 – In the Manner of the Person
310 – Let's All Be Me
312 – Poker Face
315 – Trust Circle

VERBAL

301 – Birthdays
308 – If S/he Was a Tree
311 – Name Chain
313 – Silly Me
314 – Tell Me True
316 – Turn Round

PERSONAL

301 – Birthdays
306 – Home Chase
308 – If S/he Was a Tree
309 – In the Manner of the Person
310 – Let's All Be Me
312 – Poker Face
313 – Silly Me
314 – Tell Me True

301 Birthdays

```
        X
    X       X       FOCUS   – HIGH
    X           X   SHAPE   – CIRCLE
  X             X   TIME    – 5–10 MINUTES
  X             X   ENERGY – LOW
    X           X   SHOW    – NO
      X       X     EXTRAS – NONE
        X
```

1. The players sit in a circle.
2. One player, *A*, is to have an imaginary birthday.
3. The player to the right of *A* announces what present s/he would give to *A* if money, time and possibility could be ignored.
4. Each player in turn adds a present to the list.
5. *A* then has to decide which of the presents s/he would most like to accept. (Only *one* is allowed.)
6. The player whose gift is accepted by *A* has the next birthday.

302 Blind Killer

X   X

    X   FOCUS – LOW

  X   SHAPE – GROUP WANDERING

      X   TIME   – 5–15 MINUTES

     X   X   ENERGY– MEDIUM

  X   SHOW – NO

   X   EXTRAS – BLINDFOLDS

     X

1. The players put on blindfolds and move around the room.
2. The session leader chooses one player to be the Hunter and whispers this fact to that player.
3. The Hunter tries to catch all the other players.
4. The Hunter catches someone by tapping on the 'victim's' shoulder three times.
5. The 'victim' screams and 'dies'.
6. When a player has been caught s/he may take off the blindfold and watch the rest of the chase, silently.

Note: In absence of blindfolds players may close eyes.

303 Blind Trust

	FOCUS	– LOW
XX		
	SHAPE	– PARTNERS
XX		
XX	TIME	– 5–10+ MINUTES
XX	XX ENERGY	– LOW/MEDIUM
XX	SHOW	– NO
XX	EXTRAS	– NONE

1. Everyone finds a partner, one is *A* the other *B*.
2. *A* stands still, eyes closed, with one arm held out, hand outstretched and palm downwards.
3. *B* places one finger under *A*'s outstretched palm. This is the only contact between them.
4. *A* and *B* do not speak.
5. *B* leads *A* around the room.
6. The aim is to help the 'blind' players to feel confident in their ability to move around the room when led by their partners.

Notes: Before the game *B* can have a practice by leading *A* around the room whilst talking, describing where they are in the space, and holding *A*'s arm at the hand and elbow. This will build up *A*'s confidence for the minimal contact in the actual game.

Developments. If there is time reverse the roles so that *B* experiences the fears or challenges of being led.
Then ask each pair to choose a sound which will be their call to each other. This time *A*, still with closed eyes, has to follow *B*'s call. There is no physical contact between them at all.

BLIND TRUST

304 Catch the Name

```
        X
    X           X       FOCUS  – PASSING HIGH
  X                 X   SHAPE  – CIRCLE
  X                 X   TIME   – 3–5 MINUTES
  X                 X   ENERGY – MEDIUM
   X                X   SHOW   – NO
    X           X       EXTRAS – FOOTBALL
        X
```

1. The players stand in a circle.
2. One by one the players announce their names, slowly and clearly.
3. Repeat but this time players try to remember each others' names.
4. A football is thrown from player to player across the circle.
5. Each thrower must call the name of the player to whom s/he is throwing the ball.
6. If a thrower calls the wrong name the catcher gives the correct name before continuing the game.

Note: This game is effective but can become boring if played for too long. Learning names should not become a chore. It is better to play for a few minutes at the beginning of two sessions rather than for ten minutes in one.

305 Guard and Thief

```
X  X  X  X  X  X  X  X
X     X              X     FOCUS  – SHARED HIGH
X                    X
X                    X     SHAPE  – SQUARE
X                    X
                           TIME    – 5–10 MINUTES
X                    X
                           ENERGY – LOW
X        X           X
                           SHOW   – YES
X                    X
                           EXTRAS – 2 BLINDFOLDS, KEYS
X  X  X  X  X  X  X  X
```

1. The players stand in a square.
2. Two players stand inside the square; one is the Guard the other the Thief.
3. The Guard and Thief put on blindfolds. They are moved around the square by two other players until they are standing some distance apart and are unaware of each other's position.
4. To cover the sound of this movement, the players in the square make noises with their feet.
5. While this is happening the session leader silently places a bunch of keys somewhere in the circle.
6. At a signal from the session leader the Thief tries to find the keys moving as quietly as possible because the Guard is trying to find the Thief.
7. If the Thief finds the keys s/he has won; if the Guard finds the Thief s/he has won.
8. If the Guard finds the keys s/he must leave them untouched and still try to catch the Thief.
9. If either player bumps into the wall formed by the rest of the group s/he is gently turned round to face into the square or, if s/he is moving along the line of the wall, left alone; neither player may move outside the square.

Note: Closed eyes may replace blindfolds.

GUARD AND THIEF

306 Home Chase

X	FOCUS – PASSING HIGH
X	SHAPE – GROUP MOVING
X	TIME – 3–5 MINUTES
X X	ENERGY – HIGH
X X	SHOW – NO
X	EXTRAS – NONE

1. All players announce their home town.
2. One player is the catcher, *A*.
3. *A* calls out one of the home towns and chases the player whose home it is.
4. When a player is caught s/he becomes the next chaser.
5. If the player being chased calls out another home town, the catcher changes direction and chases the new player as called.

307 I Know that Hand

```
X    X    FOCUS  – LOW
X    X    SHAPE  – TWO TEAMS
X    X    TIME   – 10–20 MINUTES
X    X    ENERGY – LOW
X    X    SHOW   – NO
X    X    EXTRAS – NONE
X    X
```

1. Everyone finds a partner, one is *A* the other is *B*.
2. All the *A*s stand in a row to form Team *A*.
3. All the *B*s stand opposite their partners, forming Team *B*.
4. The partners take each others hands and try to notice, by touch not sight, anything that will help them to recall those hands later in the game.
5. After about fifteen seconds the session leader gives a signal and all the *A*s take one step to their right. This process is repeated until team members have each returned to their original partner having 'examined' all the hands of the opposite team.
6. Team *A* members now close their eyes.
7. Team *B* move quietly away from the line.
8. At a signal from the session leader *A*s hold out their hands, their eyes still closed.
9. *B*s now go up to Team *A*, placing their hands into those of the waiting *A*s.
10. *A*s must guess whose hands they are holding.
11. Each *A* says the name of the player s/he thinks it is.
12. If the guess is correct *B* squeezes *A*'s hand and moves to another *A*.
13. After a while change over so that team *B* guess team *A*'s hands.

308 If S/he Was a Tree

```
        X
   X         X        FOCUS   – VOLUNTEER HIGH
   X         X        SHAPE   – CIRCLE
  X          X        TIME    – 5–15 MINUTES
  X          X        ENERGY – LOW
   X         X        SHOW    – NO
   X         X        EXTRAS – NONE
        X
```

1. The players sit in a circle.
2. One player, A, is asked to think of a friend in the group; A must not say the name of the friend.
3. One by one the other players ask A questions.
4. Each question begins with the words: 'If this person was a . . .' and continues 'what sort of . . . would he or she be?' The gap is filled with the name of a non-human category such as : 'a tree', 'a piece of music' and so on.
5. A answers by imagining what sort of (e.g.) tree the friend would be if personality and characteristics of the friend were transferred to that category; what sort of (e.g.) tree would s/he be?
6. When everyone has asked a question each player announces the name they think is in A's mind.
7. When all the players have had a guess A reveals the identity of the friend.

309   In the Manner of the Person

X

X		X	FOCUS	– SHARED HIGH
X		X	SHAPE	– CIRCLE
X		X	TIME	– 5–10 MINUTES
X	X			
X		X	ENERGY	– MEDIUM
X		X	SHOW	– YES
X		X	EXTRAS	– NONE

X

1. The players sit in a circle.
2. One player, *A*, leaves the room.
3. The other players choose one of their group to be the subject of the game.
4. *A* is called back into the room.
5. *A* asks four or five people to stand up and perform some imaginary task such as unwrapping a present or eating an icecream.
6. The chosen players perform the task *In the Manner of the Person* chosen by the group.
7. *A* tries to guess the name of the person being imitated.
8. *A* may change the task and/or group up to three times.

310 Let's All Be Me

```
X              X        FOCUS  – PASSING HIGH
                   X    SHAPE  – GROUP WANDERING
     X                  TIME   – 2–5 MINUTES
        X               ENERGY– HIGH
     X          X
X          X            SHOW   – POSSIBLE
                        EXTRAS – NONE
```

1. The players walk around the room.
2. One by one the players have to call out their names whilst performing a movement that represents themself.
3. For at least five seconds after a name has been called the rest of the group shout that name and copy the action.
4. Before a name is called a player must shout 'Let's all be me!'

Note: If the game is slowing down the session leader can call out names.

Variation: When a group know each other quite well players can call out the name of another person in the group whilst performing a movement that they think represents that other player.

311 Name Chain

```
            X
      X           X        FOCUS   – PASSING HIGH
       X               X   SHAPE   – CIRCLE
    X                 X     TIME    – 5–10 MINUTES
    X                 X     ENERGY – LOW
     X            X         SHOW    – NO
       X          X         EXTRAS – NONE
            X
```

1. The players sit or stand in a circle.
2. One player, A, begins the game by saying: 'Today you have met me, . . .' adding their own name to the phrase.
3. The player to the right of A continues: 'Today you have met . . . (A's name) and me, . . . (own name).
4. In this way the game continues until the last player has successfully named the whole group.

Note: This is a game for a new group.

312 Poker Face

XX

XX

XX

XX

XX

XX

XX

FOCUS – LOW
SHAPE – PARTNERS
TIME – 5–10 MINUTES
ENERGY – LOW
SHOW – NO
EXTRAS – NONE

1. Everyone finds a partner and sits opposite that partner.
2. Partners keep eye contact with each other but do not speak.
3. The session leader asks questions which are directed at everybody such as 'What sort of holiday do you think your partner would enjoy?' 'Would you like to accompany them?' 'Why?' 'Why not?' 'Why are you laughing?' and so on.
4. Partners must try to keep eye contact throughout.
5. After a while allow the players to compare notes with their partners.

313 Silly Me

```
X    X     FOCUS   – LOW
X    X     SHAPE   – TWO TEAMS
X    X     TIME    – 10–20 MINUTES
X    X     ENERGY – LOW
X    X     SHOW    – NO
X    X     EXTRAS – NONE
X    X
```

1. Everyone finds a partner, one is *A* the other *B*.
2. *A*s stand in a line, forming team *A*.
3. *B*s stand opposite their partners, forming team *B*.
4. Players tell their partners two pieces of trivial information about themselves, such as 'I always brush my hair before I wash my face', 'I talk to my potted plants – except the cactus!' and so on.
5. *A*s then take one step to their right and go through the same routine with their new partner.
6. This process is repeated until team *A* have returned to their original partners.
7. The whole sequence begins again but this time *A* says *B*'s quirks and *B* says *A*'s.

Notes: This is a useful introduction game for a new group as players find it easy to associate a name with personal information in this way. The memory part of the game can be turned into a race: *A* and *B* sit down when both have remembered correctly. This helps to time the next move.

314   Tell Me True

```
              X
        X           X        FOCUS  – PASSING HIGH
        X           X        SHAPE  – CIRCLE
      X             X        TIME   – 10–20 MINUTES
      X       X
      X             X        ENERGY – LOW
      X           X          SHOW   – NO
        X         X          EXTRAS – NONE
              X
```

1. The players sit in a circle.
2. One player, *A*, stands in the centre of the circle.
3. The player in the middle has to answer three questions.
4. The answer to each question is the name of a person in the circle.
5. *A* stands in front of the person whose name is the answer to a question.
6. The player who is the answer to a question asks *A* the next question.
7. The player who is the answer to the third question swaps places with *A* and *A* asks the new player their first question.
8. The form of the questions is always: 'Stand in front of the person who . . .', each questioner adding a different ending, such as ' . . . has the best handshake', '. . . you think cares most about their appearance', and so on.
9. If the player in the middle does not wish to answer a question the questioner must think of another one.

Trust Circle

```
    X  X
  X  X  X
    X  X        X  X
                X  X  X
  X  X          X  X
  X  X  X
    X  X
```

FOCUS – SHARED
SHAPE – CIRCLES
TIME   – 5–10 MINUTES
ENERGY – MEDIUM
SHOW – NO
EXTRAS – NONE

1. Split the group into teams of six or seven players.
2. One player, A, in each team stands with closed eyes.
3. The rest of the team form a close circle around A.
4. A gently leans backwards, with straight legs so that as s/he gradually loses balance s/he begins to fall backwards.
5. The player standing behind takes A's weight and gently pushes A back into the central upright position.
6. A repeats the process, leaning in any direction.
7. The team must take A's weight each time.
8. The team should stay silent and each player should take a turn in the centre.

TRUST CIRCLE

316 Turn Round

```
X              X        FOCUS   – LOW
X       X      X        SHAPE   – PARTNERS
        X               TIME    – 2–5 MINUTES
   X                    ENERGY – MEDIUM
   X           X        SHOW    – POSSIBLE
X              X        EXTRAS – NONE
X
```

1. Everyone finds a partner, one is *A* the other *B*.
2. *B* stands behind *A*.
3. *B* tries to say something that will make *A* turn round.
4. *B* is not allowed to touch *A* nor to shout in *A*'s ear.
5. *B* should stand at least three feet behind *A*.
6. If *B* manages to say something that would make *A* want to turn round the partners reverse roles.

Note: Can also be played using the name of the partner as the only word used.

4 IMPROVISATION GAMES

Improvisation is frequently used as a way of creating a piece of theatre in absence of a script. It is also used as a way of exploring a script. The detective work that surrounds the 'clues' offered by a script can be both enjoyable and challenging to a group if they are accustomed to questioning, creating and exploring possibilities, always wondering 'What if . . . ?'

For those working in a non-theatrical environment the same characteristics are surely desirable? Someone who sees what is but wonders how to improve it; who is faced with a seeming full stop but can find a way round it; who expected four people for dinner and can cope when eight arrive.

Improvisation is the name of the game and the following section contains games which demand quick thinking and confident response to visual, verbal and intellectual starting points.

Preparation for these games can come from any of the preceeding sections and from the *Words and Stories* section:

a) If relationships are to figure in an improvisation then encounter work is a possible introduction, games such as TRUST CIRCLE, I KNOW THAT HAND or BLIND TRUST. They could be prefaced by some partner games such as MEMORY OBJECT, MIRRORS or SPOT THE DIFFERENCE.

b) If corpsing (losing concentration and laughing) is to be avoided then try VENTRILOQUIST, DISTRACTIONS or POKER FACE.

c) If quick physical reactions are called for try FRUIT BOWL, HOME CHASE, WHAT'S THE TIME MR WOLF or LET'S ALL BE ME.

d) If the central theme is visual stimulus try CHINESE MIME, FINAL FRAME, PHOTO NEWS or PICTURE BOOK.

e) If verbal improvisation is called for try YES, NO or FORTUNATELY, UNFORTUNATELY.

f) If nerves of steel are required try FIZZ BUZZ, WHIZZ! ZOOM! or NAME EIGHT.

Games included in this section

401 – Animals
402 – At Home?
403 – Cliffhanger
404 – Copy and Change
405 – Double-take
406 – For Better or Worse
407 – Grand Opera
408 – Headlines
409 – Hot Seat
410 – In and Out
411 – Make Your Partner
412 – Opening Phrase
413 – Restoration Names
414 – Say and Do
415 – Short Story
416 – Status
417 – Swap Roles
418 – Thinks and Says
419 – Touching Scene
420 – Triangles
421 – TV Commercials
422 – What Are We Doing?

Improvisation games classified under more precise headings

EXPLORATORY

401 – Animals
402 – At Home?
407 – Grand Opera
409 – Hot Seat
410 – In and Out
411 – Make Your Partner
412 – Opening Phrase
413 – Restoration Names
414 – Say and Do
416 – Status
418 – Thinks and Says
419 – Touching Scene

PRESENTATIONAL (prepared)

405 – Double-take
408 – Headlines
410 – In and Out
413 – Restoration Names
414 – Say and Do
415 – Short Story
416 – Status
418 – Thinks and Says
420 – Triangles
421 – TV Commercials
422 – What Are We Doing?

PRESENTATIONAL (unprepared)

403 – Cliffhanger
404 – Copy and Change
406 – For Better or Worse
407 – Grand Opera
410 – In and Out
412 – Opening Phrase
414 – Say and Do
417 – Swap Roles
419 – Touching Scene
422 – What Are We Doing?

401 Animals

X					FOCUS	– LOW
			X		SHAPE	– GROUP WANDERING
		X			TIME	– 10–20 MINUTES
X	X				ENERGY	– MEDIUM
		X			SHOW	– POSSIBLE
	X		X		EXTRAS	– NONE

1. Each player finds a space in the room and lies down.
2. S/he then chooses an animal and tries to imitate the physical movements of that animal.
3. Players may not touch each other.
4. After some time has been spent working on the animal movement the players move in more human ways, that is on two feet.
5. The players must retain as many of the characteristics of their chosen animals as possible throughout the transition, producing a 'human version' of that animal.

402 At Home?

X		FOCUS	– LOW
	X	SHAPE	– INDIVIDUALS
X	X	TIME	– 5–15 MINUTES
	X	ENERGY	– LOW
X		SHOW	– POSSIBLE
	X	EXTRAS	– CHAIRS

1. Different types of chair are placed around the room.
2. Each player chooses a chair and explores different ways of sitting in/on it.
3. The session leader can help by asking questions: 'If it was a chair in your room, your favourite chair, how would you sit on it? What if it was someone else's favourite chair? In what sort of room do you think the chair would be 'at home'? How does it 'want' you to feel when you sit on it? Can you 'defeat' the chair by sitting in a way that produces the opposite feeling? . . .'
4. After a while the group are told to try out all the chairs in a similar way, without the help of questions being voiced by the session leader.
5. If time allows, group similar types of chair together to produce at least one home environment and one formal environment, more if possible.
6. One player is sent to be 'at home' and one to be 'at work' in the respective settings.
7. Other players visit them, improvising the visit and paying particular attention to the use of the chairs.

403 Cliffhanger

```
            X
    X               X        FOCUS  – SHARED HIGH
    X               X        SHAPE  – CIRCLE
   X                X        TIME   – 5–10 MINUTES
   X        X X     X        ENERGY – HIGH
     X              X        SHOW   – YES
       X            X        EXTRAS – NONE
            X
```

1. The players stand in a circle.
2. Two players, *A* and *B*, start to improvise a scene which involves some form of physical action as well as speech.
3. At a signal from the session leader the pair freeze.
4. *A* leaves the scene and rejoins the circle; *B* remains in the centre, still holding the 'frozen' position.
5. One of the other players must make sense of *B*'s position, initiating a different scene which can incorporate *B*'s starting position.
6. As soon as *B* realizes what the new situation is s/he adapts and joins in the improvisation.
7. At the next signal from the session leader the process is repeated but this time it is *B* who leaves the scene. In this way players who initiate a scene also remain for one in which they respond to a new player.
8. Any player can 'jump in', although this can prevent the slightly slower thinkers from ever having a chance to do so. Try the following:
9. After the players have practised the format the game becomes a race between the session leader and the group.
10. Immediately after giving the signal to freeze, the session leader begins counting down from ten to one.
11. If the session leader reaches zero before another player has started a new scene, the session leader has won.
12. Any player who has already had a turn must wait until the number four is reached before having another turn. (In this way the slower players have a chance without risking losing the race.)
13. The scenes are as long or short as the session leader decides, each one continuing until the signal is given.

CLIFFHANGER

404 Copy and Change

```
        X
    X           X       FOCUS  – SHARED HIGH
      X           X     SHAPE  – CIRCLE
    X               X   TIME   – 5–10 MINUTES
    X       X X         
    X               X   ENERGY – HIGH
      X           X     SHOW   – YES
        X       X       EXTRAS – NONE
            X
```

1. The players stand in a circle.
2. Two players, A and B, start to improvise a scene, involving speech and action, in the centre of the circle.
3. At a signal from the session leader the pair freeze.
4. Two more players run in and copy the position of A and B exactly.
5. A and B return to join the circle.
6. The two new players must begin a different scene that can logically start from the position they are in.
7. The scene continues until the next signal from the session leader at which the process is repeated and two new players run in.
8. The game can be turned into a race in a similar way to the last game, CLIFFHANGER, points 8–13.

405 Double-take

```
X
    X                         FOCUS   – SHARED HIGH
X                         X   SHAPE   – GROUP PLUS THREE
    X                     X   TIME    – 10–20 MINUTES
X                         X   ENERGY – MEDIUM
        X                     SHOW    – YES
    X                         EXTRAS – FEW CHAIRS, TABLE
X
```

DOUBLE-TAKE refers to any improvised scene in which one or more characters see something they were not expecting to see in the given situation. What is seen arouses an objective and therefore the impulse for action. However, the behaviour appropriate to the situation influences the manner in which the action must be undertaken and the objective pursued.

1. Three players, A, B and C prepare a setting appropriate to a given situation. They are told the place and the time of day.
2. The rest of the group are the audience and sit some distance away.
3. C is to be an 'extra' in the scene, someone whom A and B can involve as they wish.
4. A leaves the room whilst B is given some extra background information.
5. B leaves the room whilst A is given some extra background information.
6. The audience have heard all the information.
7. At any point the session leader can give warning that there are five minutes remaining in which unachieved objectives must be pursued.

Example: THE NEW COAT. All three players are told that the scene takes place at the jewellery counter of an exclusive department store. The store closes in twenty minutes. C is the assistant serving at the counter

   A is told: *You are Mrs . . . (name); you are quite well-to-do and today is your birthday. Your grown up son, whom you have not seen for some months, arrived this morning with a present – the expensive new coat which you are now wearing. You are overjoyed with it. Your husband forgot to buy you anything and has suggested that you buy some jewellery to*

match the coat. He will foot the bill. That is why you are here.
You know . . . (B), she is a leading society personality and
you would be thrilled to meet her here as opposed to at a
society 'do' where you are just another face in the crowd.

To B: You are Mrs/Lady . . . (name), a leading society
personality. You are constantly receiving invitations to
various events. You have an account with this store and are
here to return an item of jewellery for repair. You half
recognize the lady you see at the counter but cannot
remember her name. You are very interested in the coat she
is wearing. A week ago you had one stolen and it looked
remarkably like this one, in fact it was exactly the same.
Yours was the only one of its kind, made exclusively for you.

The scene opens with A arriving at the counter while B waits
outside the room. After a couple of minutes B enters and the
scene continues.

406　For Better or Worse

```
   X  X      X  X                    FOCUS   – LOW
                    X  X      X  X    SHAPE   – GROUPS
                                                OF FOUR
X  X        X  X                      TIME    – 10–20
                                                MINUTES
                                      ENERGY – MEDIUM
                                      SHOW    – YES
                                      EXTRAS – NONE
```

1. Split into groups of four players.
2. In each group there are two actors, *A* and *B*, plus two directors, one for *A* and one for *B*.
3. *A* stands facing *B*.
4. *A*'s director stands behind *B* so that s/he can be seen by *A* but not by *B*. Similarly, *B*'s director stands behind *A*.
5. *A* and *B* decide on three things: characters, a setting and whether or not the characters know each other.
6. They then start to improvise a conversation between the two characters.
7. The actors must watch out for signals from their directors.
8. If a director signals thumbs up, the actor must develop the scene in a more optimistic way.
9. If a director signals thumbs down, the opposite occurs.
10. The directors operate independently of each other.
11. If time allows reverse the roles so that actors become directors and vice versa.

407 Grand Opera

```
            X
     X           X      FOCUS  – SHARED HIGH
       X         X      SHAPE  – CIRCLE
     X           X      TIME   – 5–15 MINUTES
     X        XX        ENERGY – MEDIUM
     X           X      SHOW   – YES
       X         X      EXTRAS – NONE
            X
```

1. The players stand in a circle.
2. Two players, *A* and *B*, stand in the centre of the circle.
3. The session leader suggests a simple situation which they improvise.
4. The scene is stopped after a short while, *A* and *B* returning to join the circle.
5. Two more players enter the acting area and re-enact the scene, this time in a style suggested by the group such as grand opera, melodrama, and so on.

GRAND OPERA

408 Headlines

```
X X                    X
X XX              X   X
X                  X  X  X
     X X
   X  X  X
X  X  X
   X  X
```

FOCUS – LOW/SHARED HIGH
SHAPE – TEAMS
TIME   – 10–20 MINUTES
ENERGY– MEDIUM
SHOW   – YES
EXTRAS – NEWSPAPER

1. Split the group into teams of five or six.
2. The session leader gives each team a newspaper headline, preferably one with ambiguous meaning.
3. The team are not told what the article is about.
4. The teams are given five minutes to prepare a scene of no more than one minute which could fit the headline they have been given.
5. Each team performs its scene for the others.
6. The session leader then tells the group the headline and reads out some of the article.

Note: If there are no newspapers the session leader can make up likely headlines, leaving out the part of the game that relates to the original articles.

409 Hot Seat

```
X  X            FOCUS  – LOW
         X      SHAPE  – PARTNERS/GROUPS
     X  X       TIME   – 5–15 MINUTES
   X  X         ENERGY – LOW
 X  X       X   SHOW   – POSSIBLE
   X        X   EXTRAS – NONE
```

1. Split the group into pairs or small groups.
2. One player in each group, *A*, is questioned by the other player(s).
3. *A* answers in role, either as a newly created character or as a well rehearsed one.
4. By questioning, the group help *A* to develop a picture of the character s/he is playing.

HOT SEAT

410 In and Out

```
        X
   X         X        FOCUS  – PASSING HIGH
  X          X        SHAPE  – CIRCLE
 X           X        TIME   – 5–10 MINUTES
 X     X
 X           X        ENERGY – MEDIUM
  X          X        SHOW   – YES
   X         X        EXTRAS – NONE
        X
```

1. The players stand in a circle.
2. One by one the players cross the circle.
3. Each player imagines that s/he is moving from one environment into another, in which s/he stays for at least ten seconds. S/he then moves out of that environment into another.
4. Only the moves, in from and out to, indicate the nature of the first and third environments.
5. The audience tries to guess where the player has come from, where s/he is and where s/he is going to.

411 Make Your Partner

XX   X
        X

   X
   X
      XX

X
X
   X
   X

FOCUS   – LOW

SHAPE   – PARTNERS

TIME   – 5–15 MINUTES

ENERGY– MEDIUM

SHOW   – POSSIBLE

EXTRAS – NONE

1. Everyone finds a partner, one is *A* the other *B*.
2. *A*s are given two tasks: they must make their partners *do* something, such as scratch their noses and they must make them *talk* about something, such as holidays.
3. *B*s are given a similar challenge, for example to make their partners sit on the floor and talk about sport.
4. Neither *A*s nor *B*s must hear each others' instructions.
5. Each pair now begins a conversation.
6. The winners are the players who first succeed in their tasks.
7. Physical force is not allowed.

412 Opening Phrase

```
XX          X
            X    FOCUS  – LOW
                 SHAPE  – PARTNERS
       X
       X         TIME   – 5–15 MINUTES
            XX
                 ENERGY – LOW
  X
  X              SHOW   – POSSIBLE
       XX
                 EXTRAS – NONE
                 X
                 X
```

1. Everyone finds a partner, one is *A* and the other *B*.
2. *B*s and the session leader leave the room.
3. The session leader gives the *B*s an ambiguous opening phrase, such as 'There are twenty of them'.
4. *B*s then enter the room and say the phrase to their partners in whatever way they wish.
5. *A*s must respond as if they know what *B* is speaking about but must not introduce facts which would pin down the subject.
6. Each pair continues for as long as possible without pinning down what it is they are talking about.
7. As some pairs drop out they are given individual phrases with which to interrupt the remaining players.
8. When interrupted, players must respond to the interjection as if they know what it means and incorporate it into their improvisation.

413   Restoration Names

```
   X                   X        FOCUS  – LOW
            X                   SHAPE  – GROUP
            X                   TIME   – 5–15 MINUTES
                 X              ENERGY – MEDIUM
   X                   X   X    SHOW   – POSSIBLE
                                EXTRAS – NONE
```

1. Each player chooses or is given a name which implies a description of character – as in Restoration comedies with names such as Pinchwife and Lady Fidget.
2. The players are given a situation such as an audition.
3. They improvise the scene, each acting in accordance with the name s/he has chosen.

414   Say and Do

```
   XX              X
                   X      FOCUS  – LOW
                          SHAPE  – PARTNERS
        X
        X          XX     TIME   – 5–15 MINUTES
                          ENERGY– MEDIUM
    X
    X                     SHOW   – POSSIBLE
                   X
                   X      EXTRAS – NONE
```

1. Everyone finds a partner, one is *A* the other *B*.
2. *A* tells a short story to *B*.
3. *A* is then given a task to do, such as to count the tiles on the floor/ceiling/wall.
4. Whilst attempting the task *A* must repeat the story.
5. *B* then tells *A* if and how the story changed.
6. Reverse roles.

415 Short Story

```
X X X
  X X                      X X   FOCUS   – SHARED HIGH
                           X X   SHAPE   – TEAMS
                             X   TIME    – 15–30 MINUTES
  X X                            ENERGY – MEDIUM
X X X      X X X                 SHOW    – YES
             X X X               EXTRAS – NONE
```

1. Before the game begins the players must create the material that is to be edited.
2. The whole group improvises a situation for about five or ten minutes, such as a courtroom, shop etc.
3. The session leader stops the improvisation and divides the group into teams of five or six.
4. Each team is given five to ten minutes to prepare a shorter version of the scene, no longer than one minute.
5. The teams are free to take any aspect of the original improvisation and to adapt it in any way. They may use any style of presentation.
6. Each team presents their 'short story' to the other players.

416 Status

Variation one:

X		XX	FOCUS	– LOW
X			SHAPE	– PARTNERS
	X		TIME	– 5–10 MINUTES
	X		ENERGY	– MEDIUM
XX		X	SHOW	– POSSIBLE
		X	EXTRAS	– NONE

1. Everyone finds a partner.
2. Each player chooses a status from one (low) to ten (high).
3. The pairs improvise, trying to maintain their status.
4. At a signal from the session leader the players try to increase or decrease their own status.
5. At another signal from the session leader they try to become higher or lower status than their partners.

Variation two:

X X		X	FOCUS	– LOW	
X		X X	SHAPE	– GROUPS OF THREE	
	X X		TIME	– 5–15 MINUTES	
	X	X	ENERGY	– MEDIUM	
X		X	SHOW	– POSSIBLE	
X X		X	EXTRAS	– NONE	

1. Split the group into threes.
2. In each group the players agree a number one (high status), a number two (medium status) and a number three (low status).
3. Each group improvises a scene in which number three is alone.
4. After a minute number two enters.
5. After two minutes number one enters.

417   Swap Roles

```
XX                          X
                            X
                                    FOCUS   – LOW
                    X               SHAPE   – PARTNERS
                    X
                            XX      TIME    – 5–10 MINUTES
            X                       ENERGY – MEDIUM
            X
                            X       SHOW    – POSSIBLE
                            X
                                    EXTRAS – NONE
XX
```

1. Everyone finds a partner.
2. Each pair begins to improvise a scene.
3. At a signal from the session leader the players swap roles
   with their partners before continuing their scene.

418 Thinks and Says

X X		X	FOCUS – LOW
X X		X X	SHAPE – GROUPS OF FOUR
	X X	X	TIME – 5–15 MINUTES
	X X		ENERGY – MEDIUM
			SHOW – POSSIBLE
			EXTRAS – NONE

1. Split the group into fours.
2. In each group there is an *A*, a *B*, a shadow for *A* and a shadow for *B*.
3. The shadows are to voice what *A* and *B* really think as opposed to what they actually say.
4. *A* and *B* agree on their characters and begin to improvise a scene.
5. Both *A* and *B* have to pause before they speak in order to give their shadows time to react to the previous statement/action.
6. After *A*'s first line *B*'s shadow voices what *B* thinks before *B* says anything.
7. Then *B* says something and *A*'s shadow responds before *A* speaks.
8. If time allows reverse roles so that *A* and *B* play shadows.

Rehearsal note: If actors are working on a learned script in a way that requires an understanding of subtext then this exercise can be useful. As an acting exercise in this context no shadows are needed, each character voicing its own thoughts as an aside before speaking a line.

THINKS AND SAYS

419 Touching Scene

```
XX          X
            X        FOCUS  – LOW
                     SHAPE  – PARTNERS
XX          X
            X        TIME   – 5–10 MINUTES
                     ENERGY – MEDIUM
   X
   X                 SHOW   – POSSIBLE
                  X
                  X  EXTRAS – NONE
```

1. Everyone finds a partner, one is *A* the other *B*.
2. Each pair improvises a scene.
3. *A* must find a way of touching *B* every time s/he speaks; the moves must be appropriate to the scene.
4. At a signal from the session leader the partners try to touch each other at every line.
5. At another signal from the session leader *B* tries to touch *A* but *A* tries to avoid *B*.

TOUCHING SCENE

420 Triangles

```
X
    X                   FOCUS   – SHARED HIGH
X
                        SHAPE   – GROUP PLUS THREE
    X
        X     X     TIME      – 10–20 MINUTES
X           X     ENERGY – MEDIUM
    X       X     SHOW      – YES
X
                        EXTRAS – FEW CHAIRS, TABLE
    X
```

1. Three players, *A*, *B* and *C* are given characters, each of whom know the other two, for example through working or living near each other.
2. The three players prepare a setting appropriate to a situation in which the three characters could meet.
3. The rest of the group are the audience and sit some distance away.
4. *A* and *B* leave the room while *C* is given some extra background information.
5. *A* and *B* are also given extra information with the other two players out of the room during each briefing.
6. An essential part of the briefings is to establish that *A* wishes to be alone with *B* who wishes to be with *C* who wishes to be with *A*. None of the characters are aware of each others' feelings.
7. The audience have heard all the information.
8. The three players then improvise the given scene.

Example: The scene is set in *A*'s home. The three characters work together on a newspaper. *A* and *B* have worked there for years and are doing very well, *A* as a reporter and *B* as a photographer. *C* is younger and has only just started work, as an office junior.

A is told: *You have a deadline tomorrow for an article you have written. B has done the photographs but had not finished developing them when you left work. S/he said s/he would call round with them within the hour so you are waiting at home. You actually wish that B would spend the whole evening with you as s/he has been the object of your secret admiration for some time now. You will try to pursue this objective but must not risk losing A's friendship altogether. You know C as s/he is the office junior. S/he has been speaking to you occasionally about your work, as juniors in journalism do, and last week borrowed some of your records. S/he will return them this evening.*

B is told: You have a deadline tomorrow for an article written by A with photographs by you. You are late with the photographs and have offered to take them to A's home after work so that the deadline is not missed. When you arrive you find that C is there which pleases you enormously. You have nothing better to do with the rest of the evening and had been half-hoping A might suggest a working dinner. Things are looking up though because you have noticed the new junior round the office. S/he would be much more fun to spend the evening with.

C is told: You are determined to be a famous reporter when you are older. At the moment A is your hero because s/he is the best reporter on the newspaper you are working with. You have been trying to emulate A as much as you can, noticing what s/he has for lunch, how s/he speaks on the phone and so on. Last week you actually managed to borrow some records from A which has given you an idea of the sort of music s/he likes. You are going to return the records tonight and have chosen to take them to A's home so that you can see how a top reporter lives at home. You are fascinated by the furnishings, the colour scheme, the whole life-style you find there. You arrive first. (Tell B to enter the scene three minutes later.)

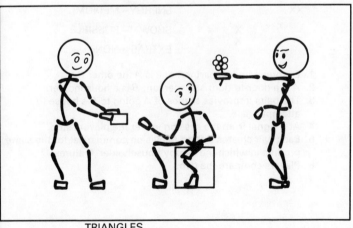

TRIANGLES

421 TV Commercials

Variation one:

```
X  X  X          X  X        FOCUS  – SHARED HIGH
X  X  X             X  X  X   SHAPE  – TEAMS
          X                   TIME   – 10–20 MINUTES
       X  X  X                ENERGY – MEDIUM
          X  X                SHOW   – YES
                              EXTRAS – NONE
```

1. Split the group into teams of five or six.
2. Each team chooses a product to promote.
3. The teams have five minutes to create a commercial for their products.
4. The teams present their commercials.
5. The group discusses which product they would want to buy as a result of the commercials.

Variation two:

```
X                   XX       FOCUS  – LOW
X
          X                  SHAPE  – PARTNERS
          X
                X            TIME   – 10–15 MINUTES
                X
   XX                        ENERGY – MEDIUM
             X               SHOW   – POSSIBLE
             X               EXTRAS – NONE
```

1. Everyone finds a partner, one is *A* the other *B*.
2. *A* is a door-to-door salesperson; *B* is a householder.
3. The pairs improvise scenes of *A* going to *B*'s house to attempt a sale.
4. At a signal from the session leader the players stop.
5. Each pair creates a short television commercial for the same product in which the 'happy householder' features.
6. Players compare the two.

128

422　What Are We Doing?

```
X  X
X  X  X
X  X
X              X  X
            X  X
        X  X  X
        X
```

FOCUS　– SHARED HIGH
SHAPE　– TWO TEAMS
TIME　　– 10–20 MINUTES
ENERGY– MEDIUM
SHOW　– YES
EXTRAS – NONE

1. Split the group into two teams.
2. Each team prepares a 'statue picture' of a social situation, such as fun on the beach, street life etc.
3. One team present their 'frozen' picture.
4. The other team copies the picture exactly and holds the freeze.
5. The first team move away.
6. The second team start a scene that could begin from that position.
7. At a signal from the session leader the scene stops.
8. The first team take up their original position and play the scene they had intended the picture to be.
9. Repeat the process for team two's picture.

5 WORD AND STORY GAMES

Story-building serves many purposes: it can provide material for a presentation; it can aid language development; it can stimulate imagination, quick thinking and improvisation; it can provide endless characters, situations and events for use in other work.

All the games in this section are to do with words or stories. Most of the story games involve creating new stories which can be daunting for a player who is not yet confident in the group. When I first started playing story games a common instruction was:

> Starting with me and going round to the right, each person must add another bit to the story . . . Once upon a time there was a tree that had been struck by lightning . . .

Those who enjoyed the challenge of story-building still felt nervous as the story plodded inevitably towards them. Those who were already nervous suffered blind panic resulting in total silence when their turn came, their vocal chords paralysed by expectation. Even when a story does emerge from such a method it tends to be boring, each part pre-planned as a way of saving face for each storyteller.

My first move away from this method was to play CATCH A STORY in which the player holding the ball tells the next part of the story, however short or long that may be. The focus is on the ball so a nervous player can throw the dreaded object away immediately; no embarrassed silences, just a mental note for the session leader as s/he notices those who find such situations difficult.

The story games in this section represent a number of different ways to create the most interesting story possible. All the games demand careful listening and verbal improvisation so appropriate preparatory games should be chosen:

a) For invention, prepare with FRUIT BOWL, LOOK UP, LOOK DOWN or GRANNY'S FOOTSTEPS, moving onto BLIND PICTURES, IN THE MANNER OF THE WORD or SOUND PICTURES.

b) If more concentrated listening is required then try LOST CHORD, EYE FOR A TOOTH, GUESS THE LEADER or RED BALL, YELLOW BALL.

c) If vocal chords need loosening up try APPLAUSE, CONDUCTOR or HAPPY FAMILIES, followed by MEMORY OBJECT, ALIBI or VENTRILOQUIST.

d) If the players are familiar with improvisation or the leader wishes to develop their ability to use it try CLIFFHANGER, COPY AND CHANGE or HEADLINES as a more creative way into story-building.

Games included in this section

501 – Catch A Story
502 – Chalk Story
503 – Chinese Stories
504 – Colour the Story
505 – Final Frame
506 – Fortunately, Unfortunately
507 – Hobbyhorse
508 – Instant Story
509 – Just a Minute
510 – Lateral Stories
511 – Name Eight . . .
512 – New Song for Old
513 – Next Line?
514 – Photo News
515 – Picture Book
516 – Walkie Talkie

Word and story games classified under more precise headings

WORD GAMES

506 – Fortunately, Unfortunately
507 – Hobbyhorse
509 – Just a Minute
511 – Name Eight . . .
512 – New Song for Old
513 – Next Line?
516 – Walkie Talkie

STORIES

501 – Catch a Story
502 – Chalk Story
503 – Chinese Stories
504 – Colour the Story
505 – Final Frame
506 – Fortunately, Unfortunately
508 – Instant Story
510 – Lateral Stories
514 – Photo News
515 – Picture Book

VERBAL

501 – Catch a Story
502 – Chalk Story
503 – Chinese Stories
504 – Colour the Story
506 – Fortunately, Unfortunately
507 – Hobbyhorse
508 – Instant Story
509 – Just a Minute
510 – Lateral Stories
511 – Name Eight . . .
512 – New Song for Old
513 – Next Line?
516 – Walkie Talkie

PHYSICAL

501 – Catch a Story
502 – Chalk Story
505 – Final Frame
512 – New Song for Old
513 – Next Line?
514 – Photo News
515 – Picture Book
516 – Walkie Talkie

LISTENING

501 – Catch a Story
503 – Chinese Stories
504 – Colour the Story
506 – Fortunately, Unfortunately
507 – Hobbyhorse
510 – Lateral Stories
513 – Next Line?

501 Catch a Story

```
        X
  X            X      FOCUS  – PASSING HIGH
  X            X      SHAPE  – CIRCLE
X                X   TIME    – 5–10 MINUTES
X                X   ENERGY – MEDIUM
  X            X      SHOW   – NO
    X          X      EXTRAS – FOOTBALL/SOFT OBJECT
        X
```

1. The players stand in a circle.
2. A football (or any soft object) is thrown across the circle from player to player.
3. The first player to hold the ball starts to tell a story, stopping as soon as s/he throws the ball to someone else.
4. Each player who catches the ball must add something to the story before throwing it on to the next player.

502   Chalk Story

```
      X
    X
   X            FOCUS   – PASSING HIGH
  X             SHAPE   – GROUP
  X        X    TIME    – 5–10 MINUTES
  X             ENERGY – LOW
  X             SHOW    – NO
   X            EXTRAS – LARGE BLANK PAPER/PEN
    X
```

1. Attach a large piece of blank paper to a wall.
2. Divide the paper into sections.
3. The players gather around the paper.
4. One player, *A*, is given a drawing instrument such as a crayon, pen or piece of chalk.
5. *A* draws the first frame of a story on the paper, telling the story as s/he does so.
6. *A* passes the chalk to another player who adds the next frame and continues the story.
7. Continue until the paper is completely covered.

503 Chinese Stories

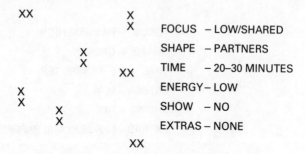

FOCUS   – LOW/SHARED

SHAPE   – PARTNERS

TIME   – 20–30 MINUTES

ENERGY – LOW

SHOW   – NO

EXTRAS – NONE

1. Everyone finds a partner, one is *A* the other *B*.
2. *A* has *four* minutes in which to tell a story to *B*.
3. The story must be created by *A*.
4. After four minutes the session leader signals for the players to stop.
5. *A* remains seated while *B* goes to join another *A*.
6. *B* now has *three* minutes in which to *retell* the story s/he has just heard.
7. At a signal *B* stops and *A* joins another *B* to retell the story s/he has just heard, this time in *two* minutes.
8. The process is repeated twice more, *B*s telling *A*s a *one* minute version and *A*s telling *B*s a *thirty-second* version.
9. The players come together and sit in a circle.
10. Each *B* tells the group the thirty-second story which s/he has just heard.
11. The player who started the story tells the group what has changed about it.

504 Colour the Story

```
                X
        X           X       FOCUS  – PASSING HIGH
        X                   X   SHAPE  – CIRCLE
    X                       X   TIME   – 5–10 MINUTES
    X                       X   ENERGY – LOW
        X                   X   SHOW   – NO
            X               X   EXTRAS – NONE
                X
```

1. Everyone sits in a circle.
2. One player begins a story by saying a phrase or sentence, such as 'The child walked down the road.'
3. The next player repeats the opening to the story but adds a description to everything mentioned, as in 'The lonely child walked slowly down the endless road to her grandfather's shop.'
4. The next player gives the next phrase or sentence.

505 Final Frame

			FOCUS	– SHARED HIGH
X X		X	SHAPE	– TEAMS
X X		X X X	TIME	– 10–20 MINUTES
	X X X		ENERGY	– MEDIUM
	X X		SHOW	– YES
X X		X		
X X		X X X X	EXTRAS	– NONE

1. Split the group into teams of four or five players.
2. Each team is moulded into a picture (like statues) by the others.
3. The teams are given five minutes to create a scene that ends with their 'picture'.
4. Each team performs its scene to the others.

FINAL FRAME

506 Fortunately, Unfortunately

As a story game:

	X			
X		X	FOCUS	– PASSING HIGH
X		X	SHAPE	– CIRCLE
X		X	TIME	– 3–8 MINUTES
X		X	ENERGY	– LOW
X		X	SHOW	– NO
X		X	EXTRAS	– NONE
	X			

1. The players sit in a circle.
2. One player makes up the first line of a story.
3. The line must begin with 'Fortunately'.
4. The next player adds a second line, this time beginning with 'Unfortunately'.
5. The story continues around the circle in this way.
6. If time allows try a story starting with 'Unfortunately'.

As a word game:

X X X	X		FOCUS	– PASSING HIGH
X X	X X		SHAPE	– TEAMS
	X		TIME	– 5–10 MINUTES
X X X	X		ENERGY	– LOW
X X	X X		SHOW	– POSSIBLE
	X		EXTRAS	– NONE

1. Split the group into teams of four or five players.
2. One player in each group, *A*, chooses to be either an optimist, who starts every speech with 'Fortunately', or a pessimist who starts every utterance with 'Unfortunately'.
3. The rest of the group adopt the opposite characteristic; they must try to contradict *A*'s standpoint until s/he expresses their point of view.
4. *A* makes a statement prefaced with the appropriate word.
5. Any member of the team can make a contradictory contribution before *A*'s next remark, though the team are

only allowed to match each statement of *A*'s with one contribution.
6. Each team member takes a turn at being *A*.

507 Hobbyhorse

```
XX              X
                X
                    X
                    X   FOCUS  – LOW
   X                    SHAPE  – PARTNERS
   X
            X           TIME   – 5–10 MINUTES
            X
                XX      ENERGY – LOW

   X                    SHOW   – POSSIBLE
   X
                    X   EXTRAS – NONE
                    X
```

1. Each player chooses a favourite topic, one which s/he can easily talk about for some time.
2. S/he then finds a partner and they begin a conversation.
3. The players try to bring the conversation round to their own preoccupation without making themselves either obvious or discourteous.

508 Instant Story

```
                    X
         X          X      FOCUS  – LOW
         X          X      SHAPE  – CIRCLE
       X              X    TIME   – 5–10 MINUTES
       X            X      ENERGY – LOW
         X          X      SHOW   – NO
         X          X      EXTRAS – NONE
                  X
```

1. The players sit in a circle.
2. The session leader asks two questions:
   i) is our story about children or adults?
   ii) Does it start inside or outside?
3. Anyone in the group may answer.
4. If more than one answer is given to a question, every answer must be included in the story.
5. If some of the answers are contradictory they provide the session leader with the next question, 'How can this be possible?' The group must provide an explanation.
6. As the story becomes more complex the session leader repeats 'the story so far'.

509 Just a Minute

```
        X
    X       X       FOCUS  – VOLUNTEER HIGH
  X         X       SHAPE  – CIRCLE
 X           X      TIME   – 5–10 MINUTES
 X           X      ENERGY – LOW
  X         X       SHOW   – POSSIBLE
    X       X       EXTRAS – STOPWATCH/WATCH
        X
```

1. The players sit in a circle.
2. One player, *A*, is given a stopwatch, or a watch that shows seconds.
3. Another player, *B*, volunteers to make a one-minute speech.
4. *A* gives *B* a topic for the speech and gives the signal for *B* to begin.
5. *B* must speak for one minute without hesitation, deviation or repetition.
6. If any player detects one of the above faults in *B*'s performance s/he may challenge *B*.
7. As soon as a challenge is made the stopwatch is stopped or the time noted.
8. If *A* agrees with the challenge then the challenger takes over the topic and must speak for what remains of the minute.
9. Any speaker is open to challenge.
10. The player speaking when the minute is reached wins the point for that topic.

510 Lateral Stories

```
      X
    X       X        FOCUS  – LOW
    X       X        SHAPE  – CIRCLE
  X           X      TIME   – 5–10 MINUTES
    X       X        ENERGY – LOW
    X       X        SHOW   – NO
    X       X        EXTRAS – NONE
      X
```

1. The players sit in a circle.
2. The session leader gives the group a few clues towards a story.
3. The players try to discover the full story by asking questions arising from the details.
4. If the answer to a question would not help the players the session leader answers 'irrelevant'.
5. The only other answers allowed are 'Yes' and 'No'.

Examples:

Clues: Anthony and Cleopatra lie dead in a pool of water. Near them is some broken glass. What happened?
Solution: They are goldfish. Their bowl was knocked over and broke.

Clues: A woman walks into a bar and asks for a glass of water. The barman takes out a gun and points it at her. The woman says thank you and leaves. Why?
Solution: The woman had hiccups.

511 Name Eight . . .

```
            X
     X           X        FOCUS   – HIGH
   X               X      SHAPE   – CIRCLE
  X                  X    TIME    – 5–10 MINUTES
  X                  X    ENERGY – LOW
   X               X      SHOW    – POSSIBLE
     X           X        EXTRAS – SMALL OBJECT
            X
```

1. The players sit in a circle.
2. One player, *A*, sits with closed eyes.
3. A small object is passed around the circle until *A* calls 'Stop'.
4. *A* calls out a letter of the alphabet, then calls 'Go'.
5. The person holding the object must pass it on as soon as 'Go' is said.
6. As soon as s/he passes the object on, the person who was holding it must name eight things beginning with the letter chosen by *A*.
7. The players pass the object twice around the circle as quickly as possible.
8. The eight things must be named within this time.

512　New Song for Old

```
X  X  X
  X  X              X  X
                 X  X
      X  X
        X
      X  X
```

FOCUS　– SHARED LOW/HIGH

SHAPE　– TEAMS

TIME　– 15–20 MINUTES

ENERGY– MEDIUM

EXTRAS – PAPER AND PENCIL

1. Split the group into teams of four or five.
2. Each group has ten minutes to change the words of a well known song (either the same as each other or let the teams choose their own song).
3. Each team sings their 'new' song to the others.

Note: The pencil and paper are merely memory aids for the teams. If unavailable work without them.

513　Next Line?

```
            X
    X               X       FOCUS  – PASSING HIGH
      X                 X     SHAPE  – CIRCLE
    X                   X     TIME    – 3–10 MINUTES
    X           X             ENERGY – HIGH
      X                 X     SHOW   – POSSIBLE
        X               X     EXTRAS – NONE
            X
```

1. The players stand in a circle.
2. One player jumps into the circle and delivers the first line of a famous saying or quotation.
3. The first player to jump in with the next line of the saying scores a point.
4. Both players rejoin the circle.
5. Another player gives the next opening line.

Rehearsal note: This can be used as a line tester. Any character gives a line from anywhere in the play/scene and the character who has the next line must join in. The director can let each extract run for as long as s/he likes.

514 Photo News

```
X  X  X                    X
   X  X                    X  X   FOCUS  – SHARED HIGH
                           X      SHAPE  – TEAMS
                  X  X             TIME   – 10–20 MINUTES
                  X  X             ENERGY – MEDIUM
                     X             SHOW   – YES
X  X  X                            EXTRAS – NONE
   X
```

1. Split the group into teams of four or five.
2. Each team thinks of a newsworthy event.
3. The team works out two 'photographs' of the event by arranging themselves into a suitable 'freeze'.
4. When the teams are ready they show their photos to each other.
5. The players guess what events are being portrayed in the different presentations and choose the best 'photo' from each team.

PHOTO NEWS

515 Picture Book

```
X  X  X
      X            X  X
                      X  X
         X
   X  X  X
                   X  X
                X  X  X
```

FOCUS   – SHARED HIGH
SHAPE   – TEAMS
TIME   – 10–20 MINUTES
ENERGY – MEDIUM
SHOW   – YES
EXTRAS – NONE

1. Split the group into teams of four or five players.
2. Each team chooses a famous fairy story.
3. Each team prepares four group arrangements, as in PHOTO
   NEWS, which will tell the story.
4. The teams present their stories to each other.
5. The session leader calls 'Picture one; picture two' and so on
   for each team.
6. The other players guess which story it is.

PICTURE BOOK

516 Walkie Talkie

```
            X
     X           X        FOCUS   – PASSING HIGH
     X           X        SHAPE   – CIRCLE
   X               X      TIME    – 5–10 MINUTES
   X               X      ENERGY – LOW
     X           X        SHOW    – POSSIBLE
       X       X          EXTRAS – NONE
            X
```

1. The players walk round in a circle.
2. Each player chooses a lecture topic.
3. When the session leader taps a player on the shoulder s/he begins to speak aloud on that topic.
4. When the next player begins to lecture the first player stops.
5. When a player is tapped for the second time s/he must continue to lecture from exactly the point at which s/he broke off the previous time.

Variation: The players quietly talk through their lectures simultaneously. When the session leader taps a player s/he increases the volume until the next one speaks up.

INDEX OF GAMES

Page number in bold type indicates that game is illustrated.

Game name	Game number	Page
Alibi	201	54
Alley Cats	101	27
Animals	401	104
Applause	102	**28**
Arms Through	103	29
At Home?	402	105
Backs	104	30
Birthdays	301	83
Blind Killer	302	84
Blind Pictures	202	55
Blind Tag	203	56
Blind Trust	303	**85**
Catch a Story	501	134
Catch the Name	304	87
Chalk Story	502	135
Chinese Mime	204	57
Chinese Stories	503	136
Circle Chase	105	31
Cliffhanger	403	**106**
Colossus Tag	106	32
Colour the Story	504	137
Conductor	107	33
Copy and Change	404	108
Cross the Circle	108	34
Distractions	109	**35**
Double-take	405	109
Echoes	205	58
Eye for a Tooth	206	59
Final Frame	505	**138**
Find the Line	207	60
Fizz Buzz	208	61
For Better or Worse	406	111
Fortunately, Unfortunately	506	139
Fruit Bowl	110	36
Grand Opera	407	**112**
Granny's Footsteps	111	**37**
Guard and Thief	305	**88**
Guess the Leader	209	62
Happy Families	112	38

Game name	Game number	Page
Headlines	408	113
Hobbyhorse	507	141
Home Chase	306	90
Hot Seat	409	**114**
I Know that Hand	307	91
If S/he Was a Tree	308	92
In and Out	410	115
In the Manner of the Person	309	93
In the Manner of the Word	210	63
Instant Story	508	142
Just a Minute	509	143
Knee Fights	113	39
Lateral Codes	211	64
Lateral Stories	510	144
Let's All Be Me	310	94
Live Wire	114	40
Look Up, Look Down	115	41
Lost Chord	212	66
Machines	116	42
Make Your Partner	411	116
Me to You	213	67
Memory Object	214	68
Mirrors	215	**69**
Morse Code	216	70
Name Chain	311	95
Name Eight . . .	511	145
New Song for Old	512	146
Next Line?	513	147
Opening Phrase	412	117
Over Under	117	43
Photo News	514	**148**
Picture Book	515	**149**
Pirate's Gold	217	**71**
Poker Face	312	96
Puppet Strings	118	44
Queenio	119	45
Quick Feelings	120	**47**
Red Ball, Yellow Ball	218	73
Restoration Names	413	118
Say and Do	414	119
Short Story	415	120
Silly Me	313	97
Sound Pictures	219	74
Spot the Difference	220	75
Status	416	121

Game name	Game number	Page
Strings	121	**49**
Swap Roles	417	122
Tell Me True	314	98
Thinks and Says	418	**123**
Touching Scene	419	**125**
Triangles	420	**126**
Trust Circle	315	**99**
Turn Round	316	100
TV Commercials	421	**128**
Ventriloquist	221	76
Walkie Talkie	516	150
What Are We Doing?	422	129
What's the Time Mr Wolf?	122	50
Whizz! Zoom!	222	77
Wink Murder	223	78
Yes, No	224	79